THE ROMANS

David Downton
Melvyn Peavitt
Jon Nichol

CONTENTS

Basil Blackwell·Oxford

ACKNOWLEDGEMENTS

We are grateful to the following for their assistance in providing illustrations:

Aerofilms Ltd, for pages 18B, 28B, 32A and 46C
Airborne Forces Museum, for page 27C
Ashmolean Museum, for page 40B
Bath City Council, for pages 41D and 43A
B. T. Batsford, for page 46E
Keith Beavis, for page 6B
British Museum, for pages 19C, 25D, 27B, 36D and 37E
Cambridge University Collection: copyright reserved, for pages 30C and 38A
Colchester Borough Council, for pages 13E and 24B
Controller of Her Majesty's Stationery Office (crown copyright reserved), for pages 29F, 36B and 38B
Fleet Fotos, for page 34A
Greater London Council, for page 14D
Grosvenor Museum, Chester, for page 25C
Illustrated London News for page 8A
Mansell Collection, for pages 4C, 25E, 39D, 39E, 39F and 40G
R. Miket for page 43C
Mittelrheinisches Landesmuseum, Mainz, for pages 37G and 37H
Musée Archéologique de Dijon, for page 39C
Musées Nationaux, Paris, for page 22C
Museum of Antiquities of the University and the Society of Antiquities of Newcastle-upon-Tyne, for pages 21F, 28C and 29G
Museum of Archaeology and Ethnology, Cambridge, for page 37F.
Museum of London, for page 43B
National Monuments Record Air Photograph (crown copyright reserved), for pages 7E and 46E
National Museum of Antiquaries of Scotland, for page 14C

Reading Museum and Art Gallery, for pages 36A and 40G
Roman Fort Museum (Arbeia), South Shields, Tyne and Wear County Council Museums, for page 22D
Royal Commission on the Ancient and Historical Monuments of Scotland, for page 20D
Society of Antiquaries of London, for pages 1A, 7D and 8B
Mrs. Elizabeth Sorrell, for page 33B (originally published in Roman Britain, Aileen Fox and Alan Sorrell, Lutterworth Press, 1961)
Yorkshire Museum, for page 23E

Booklist

R. Mitchell	Roman Britain	Longman, 1968
T. Cairns	The Romans and their Empire	CUP, 1970
P. Connolly	The Roman Army	Macdonald, 1975
A. Sorrell	Roman Britain	Lutterworth, 1961
S.C. Boyd	Roman and Saxon Britain	Evans, 1969
J. Liversidge	Roman Britain Then and There	Longman, 1958
O. Thompson	The Romans in Scotland Then and There	Longman, 1968

The extracts from original sources have been transliterated for classroom use

---

First published 1979   © Basil Blackwell 1979

ISBN 0 631 93500 2

Reprinted 1982, 1983, 1984, 1987

Printed in Hong Kong by Wing King TongCo Ltd

INTRODUCTION

THE ROMANS provides an outline course on Britain in the time of the Romans. Throughout THE ROMANS emphasis is laid upon the handling of historical EVIDENCE. Each subject encourages the pupil to think actively about the clues the past has left behind, and on the basis of the evidence to work out his or her own ideas about the Romans and Britons.

The book is carefully arranged for class, group or individual work. Each subject is self-contained, and provides material for topic work. The questions are roughly graded for difficulty, and give scope for pupils who work at different speeds. They are carefully designed to encourage pupils to think about, and so build up their own picture of, the past.

History is made up of EVIDENCE from the past—a debate between sources. Look at one such historical CLUE below, and say what you think it is. After each point **a, b, c,** add any new thoughts you have about the clue.

a It is part of a skeleton, from the body of a dead man. Has the man been dead for a long time?

b What is in the middle of the backbone, pushing apart two of the vertebrae?

c The body was found in a shallow grave outside a British fort, Maiden Castle. The missile which killed the man was of Roman make. We know that the Romans captured Maiden Castle in 43 AD. Who do you think the man in the grave was? How did he die?

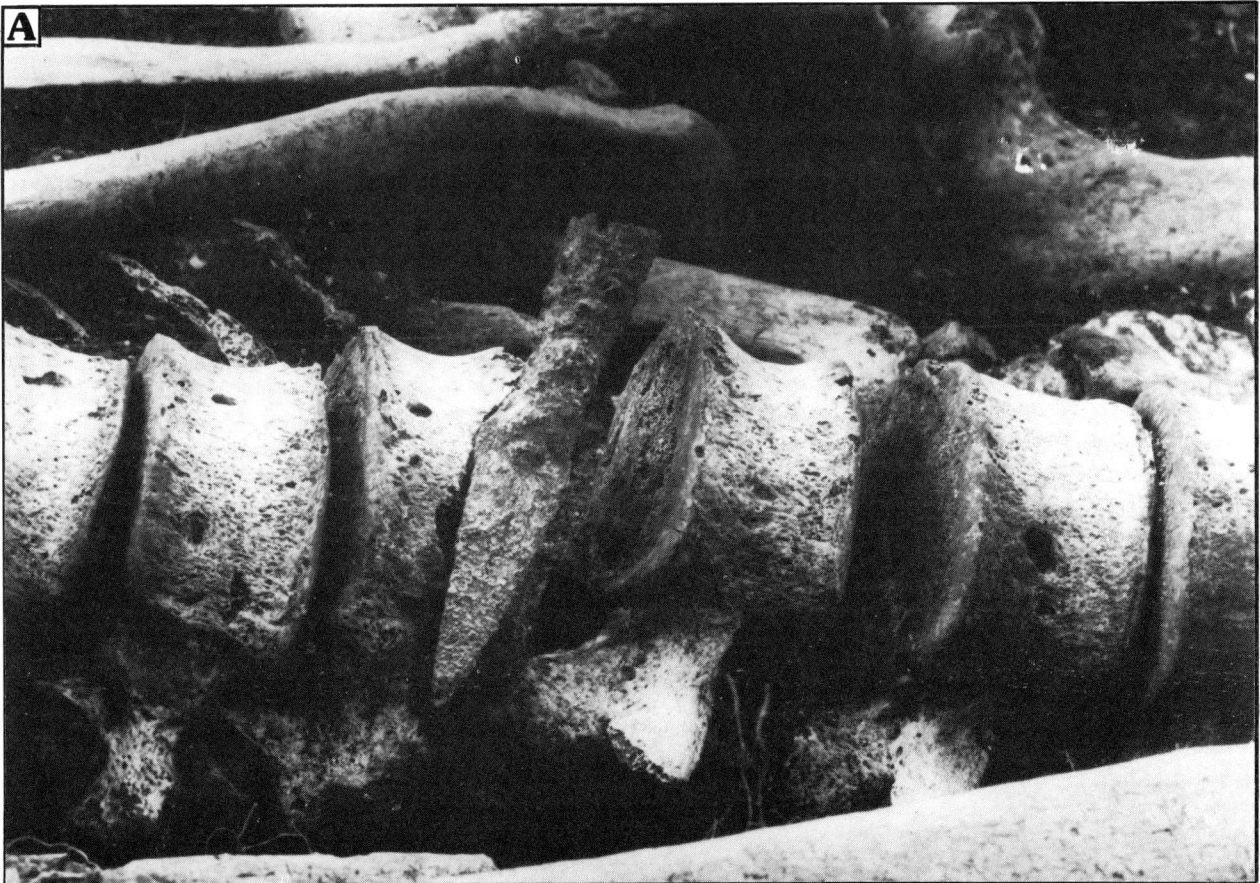

A

1

THE ISLAND

Are you going on holiday this year? If so, how will you or your parents decide where to go? What kinds of booklets, posters and other information will you look at? How about visiting the island described in **A-F**.

THE PLACE
. . . the largest island known to us, so placed that it runs parallel to both the coast of Germania to the east and Spain to the west. On its south side it actually lies within sight of Gaul. Its northern shores, with no land facing them, are beaten by a wild and open sea. **A**

The general shape has been compared to a long diamond or double-headed axe. . . Such indeed is its shape south of Caledonia. . . But when you go further north, you find a huge and shapeless mass of country, jutting out to form the most distant coastline. **B**

THE PEOPLE
We are dealing with savages. But they are of different physical types. . . The reddish hair and large limbs of the Caledonians suggest that they came from Germany; the dark, sly faces of the Silures and their curly hair, and the fact that Spain lies opposite, lead us to believe that Spaniards crossed in ancient times to live there. The people closest to Gaul likewise are similar to them. In both countries you see the same religion and ceremonies. There is no great difference in the language they speak. There is the

same rashness in rushing into unavoidable danger, and the same cowardice in avoiding it when they can. **C**

THE CLIMATE
. . . is wretched, with its frequent rains and mists, but there is no severe cold. Their day is longer than in our parts of the world. The nights are light, and in the extreme north so short that evening and morning can hardly be told apart. **D**

THE SOIL
. . . will produce good crops, except olives, vines and other plants which grow in warmer lands. They are slow to ripen, though they shoot up quickly — both facts being due to the same cause, the extreme moistness of the soil and air. **E**

THE NATURAL RESOURCES
. . . it yields gold, silver and other metals that made it worth conquering. Its seas, too, produce pearls. . . **F**

A Roman writer, Tacitus, wrote accounts **A-F** in about 100 AD. They tell us what he knew about the island.

The Romans had invaded it, defeated the tribes and begun to rule them, adding the island to the Roman Empire. It had become a Roman province, under a governor.

Tacitus governed another Roman province. He played an important part in running the Empire. His wife was the daughter of Agricola, who governed this island from 78-84 AD (see pp 16-19).

To draw map **G,** an artist used a Roman geographer's account of what the Romans knew of the world. He would have described most accurately the places that he knew best.

G The Roman world

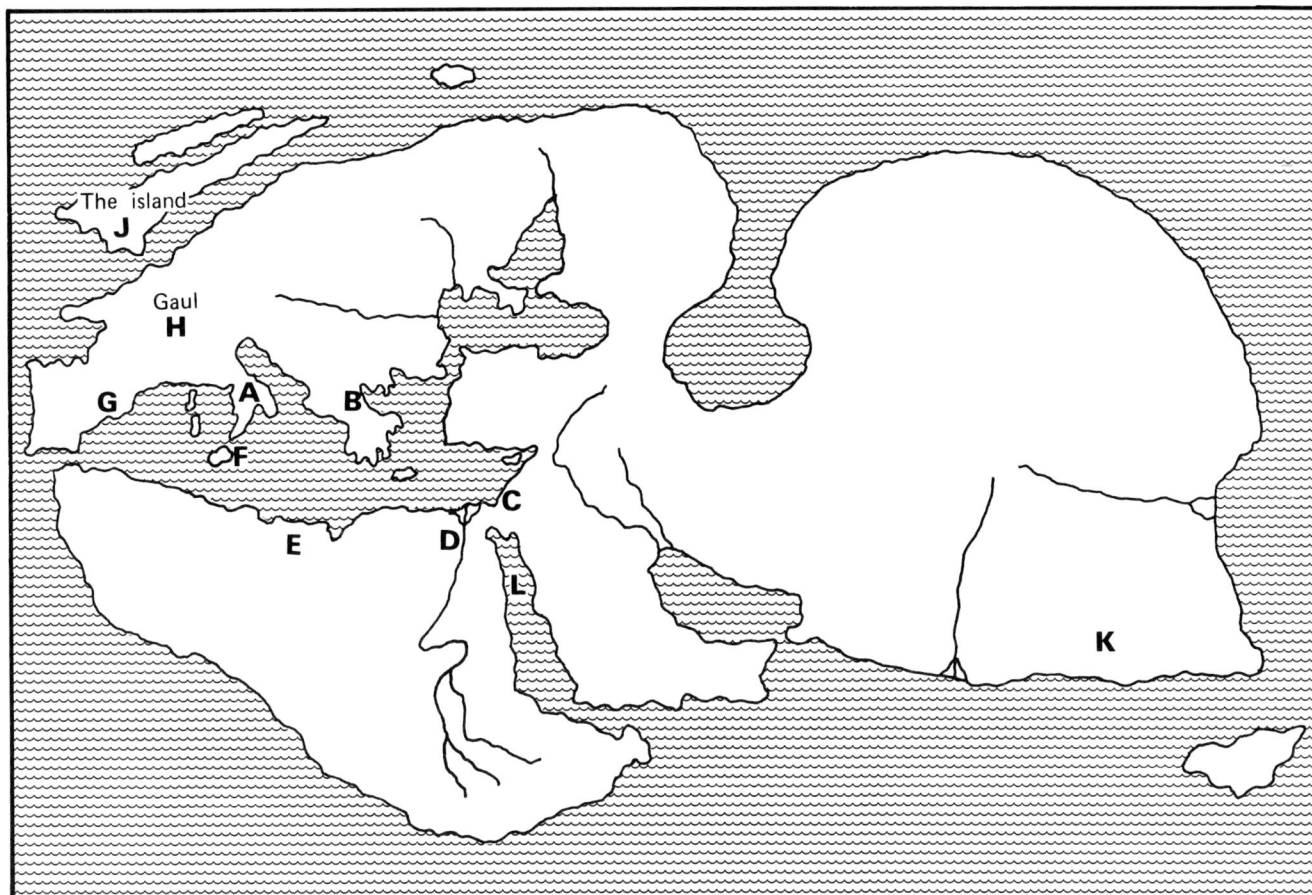

1 Use Tacitus' descriptions of the island to give brief answers to these questions.

Where was the island? What shape was it? Who lived there? What was the weather like? Why did the Romans want to visit it? Would you have liked to go there?

2 Imagine that you are a Roman travel agent. All you know about the island is given in the accounts **A-F**. Draw a poster or write a leaflet to advertise the island.

3 Use map **G** to answer these questions.
What are the modern names for the places marked **A-L** ?
Where do you think the geographer lived? You may need to look at an atlas showing Europe and Asia.

4 Can we trust Tacitus' accounts **A-F** and map **G** as historical evidence about the island?

CAESAR'S INVASION

A The Roman Empire at the death of Julius Caesar, 44 BC

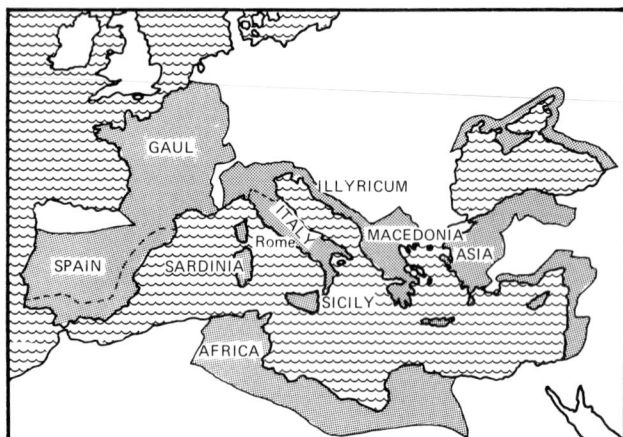

Map of the Roman Empire showing GAUL, SPAIN, SARDINIA, SICILY, AFRICA, ITALY, Rome, ILLYRICUM, MACEDONIA, ASIA

Caesar dipped his pen in the ink, as he wrote his book, called *The Conquest of Gaul*. Caesar, the Roman General Julius Caesar, re-read the letters that he had written during his wars in Gaul from 58-51 BC. See map **A**. How well the Gauls had fought! What should he say about how — and why — he had dealt with the Britons in 55 BC?

It was now near the end of summer, and winter begins early in those parts. Nevertheless I was very busy getting ready to invade Britain. I knew that in all my fights against the Gauls, they had got fresh warriors from Britain. **B**

Caesar's fleet sailed. Its ships carried about twelve thousand soldiers across the Channel. The boats, like **C**, reached Kent.

I ran my ships aground on an evenly sloping beach, with no rocks. The Britons, seeing my plan, had sent forward their horsemen, and a number of the chariots they use for fighting. The rest of their troops followed close behind. They were ready to stop us landing. We were really up against it. The size of our ships meant that they ran aground in fairly deep water. Our soldiers did not know what the beach was like. Weighed down with armour and weapons, they had to jump from the ships. Then they had to fight their way through the waves. The enemy stood on dry land or advanced only a short way into the water. Not only could they fight quite freely, but also they knew the ground. Boldly they hurled javelins and galloped their horses up and down. They were trained to do this. **D**

Caesar decided to group his smaller warships together, and charge the shore. He hoped to frighten the enemy. This might give his men time to get ashore.

C

But as our men held back, chiefly because of the deep water, the man who carried the Eagle (banner) of the 10th legion . . . cried in a loud voice, "jump down, comrades, unless you want to surrender our Eagle to the enemy. I, at any rate, mean to do my duty to my country and General'. With these words he leapt from his ship and pushed towards the enemy, carrying the Eagle. At this, our soldiers, encouraging each other not to give in to such a disgrace, jumped together from the boats. The men in the next ships, when they saw this, followed them . . . . As soon as our soldiers had reached the beach, they grimly hung on until their comrades joined them. Then they charged the enemy, who fled. **E**

Caesar's army raided deep into Kent. Then, with winter approaching, he decided to go home. Next year he returned. After a successful campaign to punish the islanders, he retired to Gaul. It was almost a hundred years — 43 AD — before a Roman army again sailed to Britain. This time the Emperor Claudius wanted to conquer Britain (pages 6-7).

???????????????????????????

1 How many men did Caesar take to England in 55 BC?

2 What problems faced them when they arrived?

3 Tell a story of the Roman landing in 55 BC, as if you were the chief of the Britons who tried to stop it. Use these words to help you: warships, banks of oars, rows of soldiers, armour, weapons, chariots, spears, javelins, shouts, screams, enemy charge, flight.

4 Imagine you were advising Caesar what to do in 54 BC. Look at map **A**, pages 6-7, and then at list **F**, to help work out what you would have suggested. After each decision *write down your reasons for making it.*

a HOW MANY FOOTSOLDIERS SHOULD HE TAKE?
From 5-10 000;
10-15 000;
15-20 000;
20-25 000.

b HOW MANY CAVALRY SHOULD HE TAKE?
From 2-4 000;
4-6 000;
6-8 000;
8-10 000.

c HOW MANY SHIPS SHOULD HE TAKE?
Each ship held about forty men. This left space for food, weapons and horses.

d WHERE SHOULD THEY LAND: BEACH **a, b** or **c**?
Last year he landed on beach **b**. It is much closer to his harbour in Gaul than the others. A major problem of the invasion is storm damage. Last year most of the boats were wrecked.

e SHOULD HE ALLY WITH THE TRINOVANTINE TRIBE?
They have asked him to help them against the most powerful British tribe, the Catuvellauni. The chief of the Catuvellauni has already killed the chief of the Trinovantines. If Caesar goes to the help of the Trinovantines, he must march a long way through enemy lands. **F**

THE ROMAN CONQUEST 1: the defences of Maiden Castle

0   50   100km

forest

a b c landing beaches

B

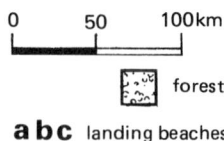

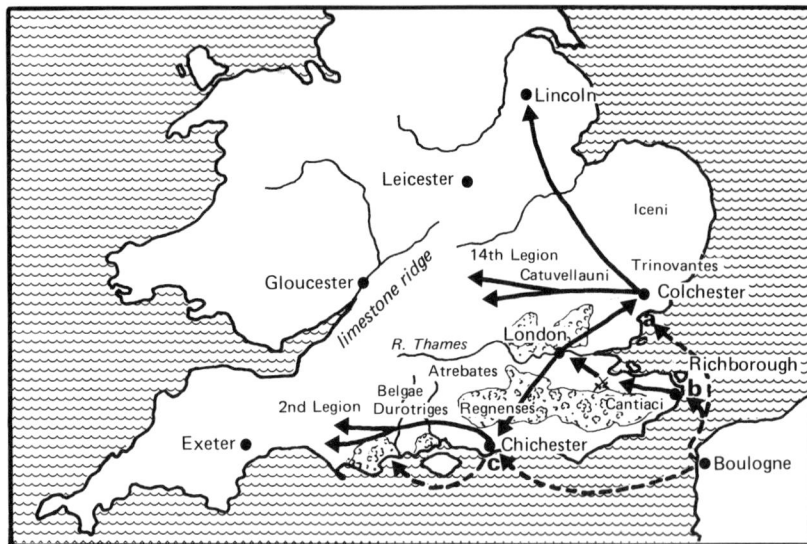

Four Roman legions landed in the south of Britain in 43 AD—map **A**. Vespasian commanded the 2nd legion. Suetonius, a Roman historian, tells us that Vespasian invaded the Isle of Wight and then landed in Dorset. In conquering the south of England, he captured twenty hill forts. One of these was Maiden Castle, in Dorset.

To make their fort, the Britons had built three banks of earth —ramparts—around a plain. **B** shows the ramparts today. Some children are trying to run up the slope. The steep ramparts made it difficult for Roman soldiers to attack, particularly those who hurled stones from slings—**C**. On level ground, a slinger could usually throw a slingstone about ninety metres.

Archaeologists found huge stores of beach pebbles around the fort, especially near the gates, where the Romans had built platforms for their slingers. In one place archaeologists dug up a store of 20 000 carefully chosen stones, **D**. The Romans collected these pebbles from an unusual long beach near Dorchester. The main roads on the plain were paved with stones.

You can see the defences of the West Gate in the aerial photograph, **E**, and on pages 10-11. They were cleverly laid out so that the attackers could not rush forward in one charge. They had to spread out in two directions.

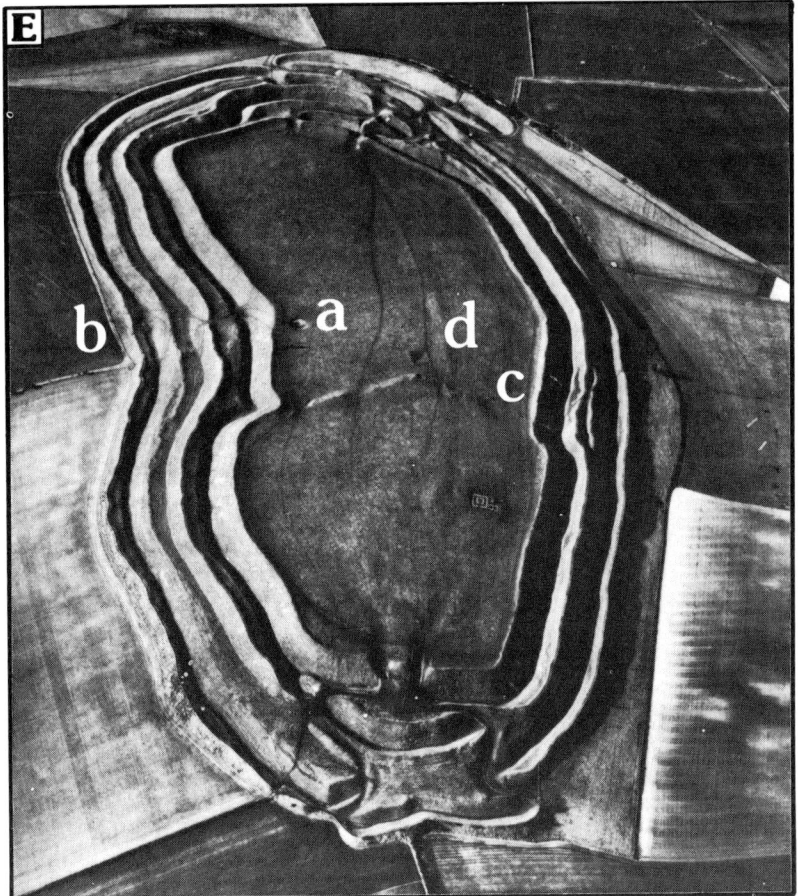

High walls of limestone blocks guarded each side of the great wooden gates. On top of the ramparts was a wall of earth nearly three metres wide. Thick wooden stakes two and a half metres tall propped up the front and back of the wall of earth.

Inside the fort, archaeologists found that the Britons no longer kept corn in underground pits, in which it seems to have rotted, but in sheds and barns.

It was vital for Vespasian to capture Maiden Castle. The Durotrigean tribe defended it. They, and the Belgaen tribe, ruled the area. To the east, one British king, Cogidumnus, had surrendered to the Romans without a fight. In return, the Romans let him go on ruling his lands. The Durotriges fought on.

?????????????????

1 What do you think it was like for the Roman soldiers who fought their way up the slopes of Maiden Castle? How did they defend themselves against the tribesmen at the top? How many ramparts did they have to storm in an attack from the west?

2 Find a map of Dorset and look for the long beach near Dorchester.

3 From **E**, work out and write down the features shown at **a, b, c** and **d**.

THE ROMAN CONQUEST 2:
the attack on Maiden Castle

An archaeologist, Sir Mortimer Wheeler, discovered from his excavations at Maiden Castle EVIDENCE about how the Romans *might* have defeated the Britons defending the hill fort. The evidence that he dug up tells us all that we know about the Roman attack: see points **a-g**. An artist drew **A** from Wheeler's evidence.

a Vespasian's legion got ready to attack, outside the East Gate.

b The Romans fired showers of arrows and spears, and catapulted stones and bolts into the British fort.

c They burnt to the ground British huts outside the East Gate and set cornfields on fire. Sir Mortimer, who had been a soldier, thought that the Romans intended to make a thick smokescreen and so cover their attack.

d The East Gate was destroyed, probably in the fighting.

e The Britons buried their dead in shallow graves in the ashes of the burnt-out huts, **B**. The bodies were all together, in any position. But next to them was a pot and a bowl or the remains of some food.

f The Britons who survived the attack buried people in the normal British way: separately, and in a curled-up position.

g Because of the way the bones of the Britons' bodies were broken, we know that they had been hacked about *after* they had been killed.

We are not sure exactly what happened at Maiden Castle. Tacitus wrote this account of an attack about fifteen years later on a similar British hill fort.

The Romans pushed forward to the parapets. The struggle there was fierce. As long as the Britons could hurl spears, rocks and arrows, they could win. The Romans advanced under a tortoiseshell formation of shields, and broke through the enemy's wall. Hand-to-hand fighting followed. The Britons fled up the hill. The Romans eagerly followed. Both auxiliaries and legionaries forced their way to the summit under a hail of spears. The Britons, without breastplates and helmets, could not hold out. The legionaries, with swords or javelins, carried all before them. The auxiliaries, with spears and swords, slaughtered the enemy. **C**

The Britons lived on in the battered fort, but after about twenty-five years moved to a new town two kilometres away, called Durnoveria—Dorchester.

Map **D** suggests the steps by which the Romans went on to conquer Britain. The map has been worked out from the small number of CLUES we have, such as Flaminius' tombstone in Wroxeter (see pages 24-25). We know that Flaminius' legion was one of those which invaded Britain in 43 AD.

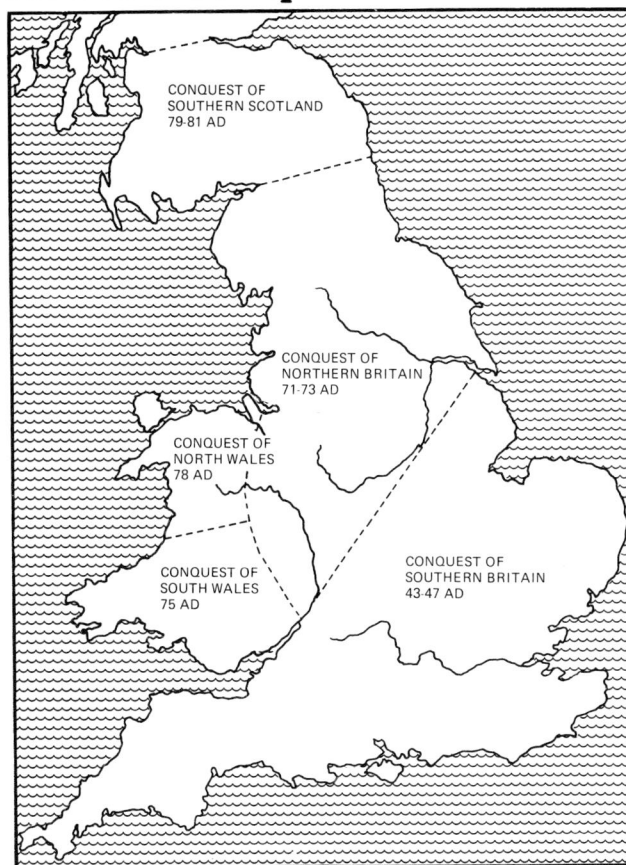

D Steps in the Roman conquest

0   150 km

CONQUEST OF SOUTHERN SCOTLAND 79-81 AD

CONQUEST OF NORTHERN BRITAIN 71-73 AD

CONQUEST OF NORTH WALES 78 AD

CONQUEST OF SOUTH WALES 75 AD

CONQUEST OF SOUTHERN BRITAIN 43-47 AD

?????????????

1 Write a story of what might have happened at Maiden Castle. To help you, use Sir Mortimer Wheeler's evidence, picture **A**, Tacitus' account—**C**, the information on pages 26-29 and these words:

Vespasian's legion, East Gate, fort, drawn up, catapults, bolts, javelins, enemy, huts, burning, roofs, shouting, screams, charge, spears, swords, fighting, bodies, capture, advance, slaughter, blood, surrender, Britons, burial.

2 What problems do you think might have faced the Roman legions in conquering Britain?

3 Can we trust Sir Mortimer Wheeler's evidence on Maiden Castle?

REBELLION 1:
Boudicca

By 61 AD, the Governor of Britain, Suetonius Paulinus, was wondering what to do next. In seventeen years the Romans had conquered or become friendly with most of the tribes. Suetonius, a soldier, wanted action. The Welsh tribes were still causing trouble. Where should he strike against them? Tacitus tells us this.

He decided to conquer the Isle of Anglesey (off the coast of North Wales), the home of a tribe of warriors, and a popular refuge for rebellious Britons. . . **A**

Anglesey was rich in corn and copper mines. So, Suetonius "ordered a number of flat-bottomed boats to be built", and ferried his army across the Menai Straits.

The Britons were ready for action. Women rushed through the ranks in a frenzy, hair waving in the wind, wearing dark cloaks and carrying flaming torches. . . The Druids stood in ranks, their hands uplifted, calling to the gods for help. . . **B**

The Druids were chief priests of all the different religions practised by British tribes. They looked after the temples and lived on gifts made to the gods. The Druids were often asked for advice by British nobles, but they were feared as well—human sacrifice was part of their religion. The Romans knew how much influence the Druids had and killed them whenever they could.

The legions (crossed to Anglesey and) charged flat out. The Britons perished in the flames they had lit. The island surrendered. . . religious woods, dedicated to devil worship and foul ceremonies, were hacked down. Here the natives had covered their altars with the blood of their prisoners and the ripped-out guts of men sacrificed to their gods.

While Suetonius made his plans to keep Anglesey under control, news arrived that Britain had revolted, and the whole province was up in arms. **C**

What had caused the rebellion? Tacitus gives us some clues.

Prasutagus, the late King of the Iceni tribe, had got together a huge treasure during his long reign. He left it in equal shares to his two daughters and the Emperor (Nero). But Roman tax collectors looted his lands, whipped his wife Boudicca and assaulted her two daughters. The Romans' slaves robbed his house. Leading members of the Iceni tribe lost their homes and lands. The relatives of the late King (Prasutagus) were made slaves. The Iceni rebelled. **D**

This was the start of Boudicca's rebellion. At St Albans, the Catuvellauni joined the rebellion, mainly because they had to hand over their lands to the Roman settlers who set up the colony there. Map **E** shows the rough boundaries between the tribes.

??????????????

1 Using the facts on these pages and Tacitus' accounts **A-D**, say why Suetonius attacked Anglesey.

2 Imagine how a Roman centurion might have felt when he entered the Druid woods and temples. Who do you think were the prisoners sacrificed on the Druid altars?

3 Why did the Iceni rebel? Do you think Suetonius was a good governor?

REBELLION 2:
Colchester

At Colchester, the Trinovantes joined Boudicca, as Tacitus tell us.

What chiefly made them angry was how the Roman veterans had behaved when they founded the colony at Camulodunum (Colchester). They treated the Britons cruelly. They drove them from their homes and called them slaves. . . Regular soldiers helped the veterans. . .

Another cause of anger was the temple built in honour of (Emperor) Claudius. In British eyes it was a symbol of everlasting slavery. The Roman priests. . . made the natives pay heavy taxes for the temple's ceremonies. **A**

The Trinovantes rebelled against the colonists and their priests. Colchester was eleven years old but had no defences. Therefore:

. . . the veterans sent to Catus Decianus, the chief tax-collector, for help. Two hundred men, not all properly armed, were all he could spare. The colony had only a handful of its own soldiers. The temple was strongly fortified and they hoped to make a stand. . . The Trinovantes destroyed the colony by fire and sword. The temple, after a siege of two days, was stormed. **B**

The rebels showed no mercy, but massacred every man, woman and child.

Map **C** shows the problems which faced the Romans. The nearest legions were over a hundred and sixty kilometres away, in Lincoln, Gloucester and Wales. Hearing the news of the attack on Colchester, the

0   100km

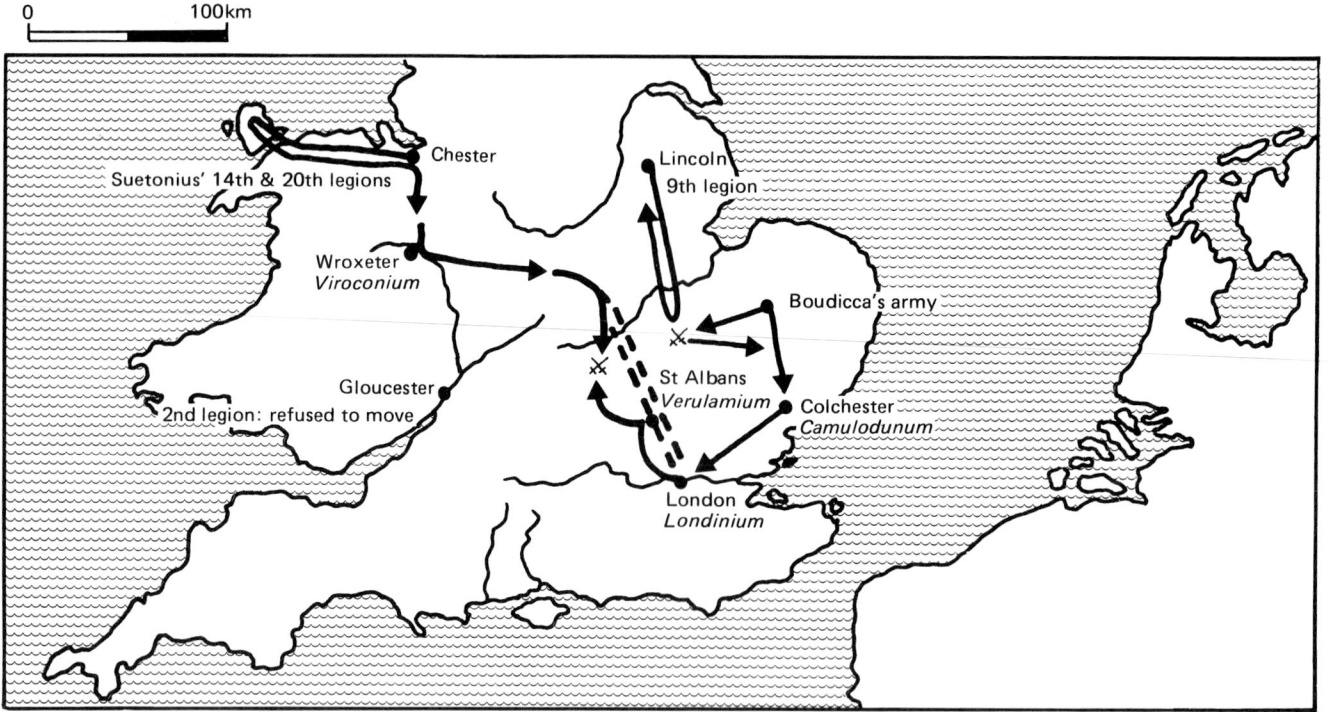

Suetonius' 14th & 20th legions

Chester

Lincoln
9th legion

Wroxeter
Viroconium

Boudicca's army

Gloucester

2nd legion: refused to move

St Albans
Verulamium

Colchester
Camulodunum

London
Londinium

H

. . . 9th legion (from Lincoln) marched to the relief of that place. The Britons, delighted with their success, advanced to fight. The legion was heavily defeated, and its footsoldiers cut to pieces. **D**

Only the cavalry of the 9th escaped. **E** shows a tombstone in the Roman cemetry outside Colchester. It is from the grave of a junior cavalry officer of the 9th legion. The Roman soldier on horseback is riding over a bearded British tribesman.

Meanwhile, Suetonius marched from Anglesey

. . . to London, not called a colony, but the chief home of merchants and a great centre of trade and business. . . There he meant to fight, but thinking his army too small, he decided to leave. **F**

??????????

1 Where was the nearest legion to Colchester? If it could march thirty kilometres a day, how long would it take to get to the town?

2 Why do you think the Romans had not fortified Colchester?

3 Why might the 9th legion have been defeated?

4 Two clues told archaeologists what the rebel Britons might have done to the tombstone. What are they?

5 Look carefully at map **C**, and the evidence on these pages. What would you advise Suetonius to do after leaving London? Put plans **a-d** in your order of choice, and give your reasons.

> **a** March to join the 2nd legion and wait for help from Gaul.
>
> **b** Try to make an agreement with Boudicca.
>
> **c** Fortify a camp near London, and wait for the 2nd legion and other troops to come to your help.
>
> **d** March after the enemy army, and force a decisive battle.

6 **G** shows scraps of metal excavated in Colchester. These suggest that the colonists had tried to make their own armour. Archaeologists have also excavated two bent swords. What can you identify in **G**.

7 **H** shows the wall of a wattle and daub house which was baked hard in the fire when the rebels attacked Colchester. How do archaeologists know that this wall was burnt during the Roman occupation?

13

Of all who stayed behind (in London) because of old age, the weakness of their sex, or the love of their homes, not one escaped the barbarians' rage. The people of St Albans . . . were likewise put to the sword. The instinct of a savage people always makes them search for plunder. They avoided our soldiers and attacked where they knew no one would fight back. The number massacred was at least 70 000. All were citizens or allies of Rome. **A**

REBELLION 3:
defeat

Tacitus then tells us how Suetonius, the Roman governor, got ready to fight Boudicca. His account is our source of information about the battle.

The 14th legion joined Suetonius, with the veterans of the 20th legion and auxiliaries from forts nearby. His army added up to little more than ten thousand men . . . he decided to fight the crucial battle. Because of this, he chose a spot circled by woods. It had a narrow entrance and dense trees behind. So he had no fear of an ambush. The enemy, he knew, had to come at him from the front across an open plain. He drew up his soldiers in this order. The legions were close together in the centre. The lightly-armed troops were kept at the back to fight when needed. The cavalry were on the wings.

A huge number of Britons came to the battlefield. They did not draw up in clear lines of fighters. Separate bands and whole tribes rushed up and down shouting. So sure were they of winning, that they put their wives in carts on the edge of the plain. There they could see the battle and admire the Britons' amazing bravery. Boudicca drove through her army with her two daughters in a war chariot. (See **C** and **D**) **B**

Tacitus goes on to say that both Boudicca and Suetonius encouraged their armies to destroy the enemy. Then:

The battle began. The Roman legions formed lines. The narrow passage (into the clearing) slowed down the enemy attack. But the Britons advanced fiercely, and threw their spears with deadly results. Then the Romans rushed forward in a wedge. The auxiliaries followed with as much keenness. Straight away the cavalry charged the enemy. With their lances they killed all who dared to make a stand. The Britons fled, but got tangled up in the waggons at the rear. A dreadful slaughter followed. Neither men nor women were spared. Some writers say that at least 80 000 Britons were killed. The Romans lost about 400 men. About the same number were wounded. Boudicca took poison and killed herself. **E**

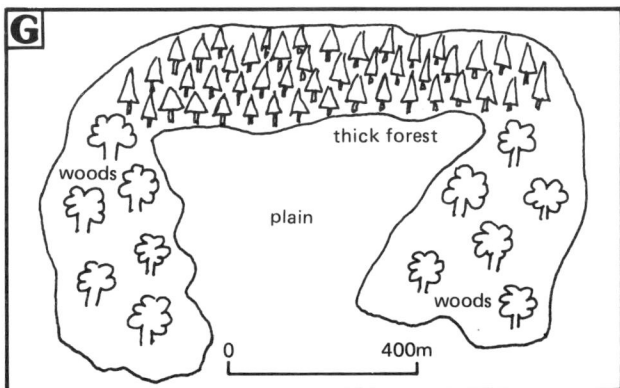

Boudicca was not the only one to commit suicide. The Commander of the 2nd legion had refused to join Suetonius.

As soon as he heard of the brave deeds of the 14th and 20th legions, he was stung by shame. He fell upon his sword and died on the spot. **F**

1 Use Tacitus' story, and your own drawing of **G**, to mark the positions, at the battle's start, of:

a the Roman legions, auxiliaries and cavalry;

b the British soldiers;

c the British carts.

Then use arrows to show how the battle went:

a the British attack;

b the Roman charge;

c the British flight.

2 Organizing a rebellion is difficult. So many things must go right. Pretend that you want to organize a rebellion in this country today. **H** lists the groups that you would need to control. Mark these in order of importance, from 1-10. Write an account of your reasons.

H

police	
navy	
television, radio, newspapers	
army	
air force	
industry	
farming	
post and telephones	
government	
railways, airports, ports	

3 As if you had been with Suetonius, write up a diary of what happened at the different stages of the rebellion.

AGRICOLA 1:
a Roman governor

Agricola is a good example of the governors who helped rule the countries that the Romans conquered—the Roman Empire. Tacitus tells us this.

He learnt his job as a soldier in Britain, and pleased the Governor, Suetonius Paulinus, a hard-working and sensible officer. Suetonius chose Agricola as one of his own officers, to see if he was up to the mark . . . Agricola got to know the province, and became known by the soldiers . . . He learned from the experts . . . **A**

Agricola fought fiercely against the Britons.

. . . Roman veterans had been massacred, new towns burned to the ground, armies cut off. They had to fight for their lives before they could think of victory . . . Everything helped give the young Agricola fresh skill, experience and ambition. **B**

He took part in the attack on the Druids in Anglesey, and in putting down Boudicca's revolt—pages 14-15. Tacitus tells us about the next steps in Agricola's career.

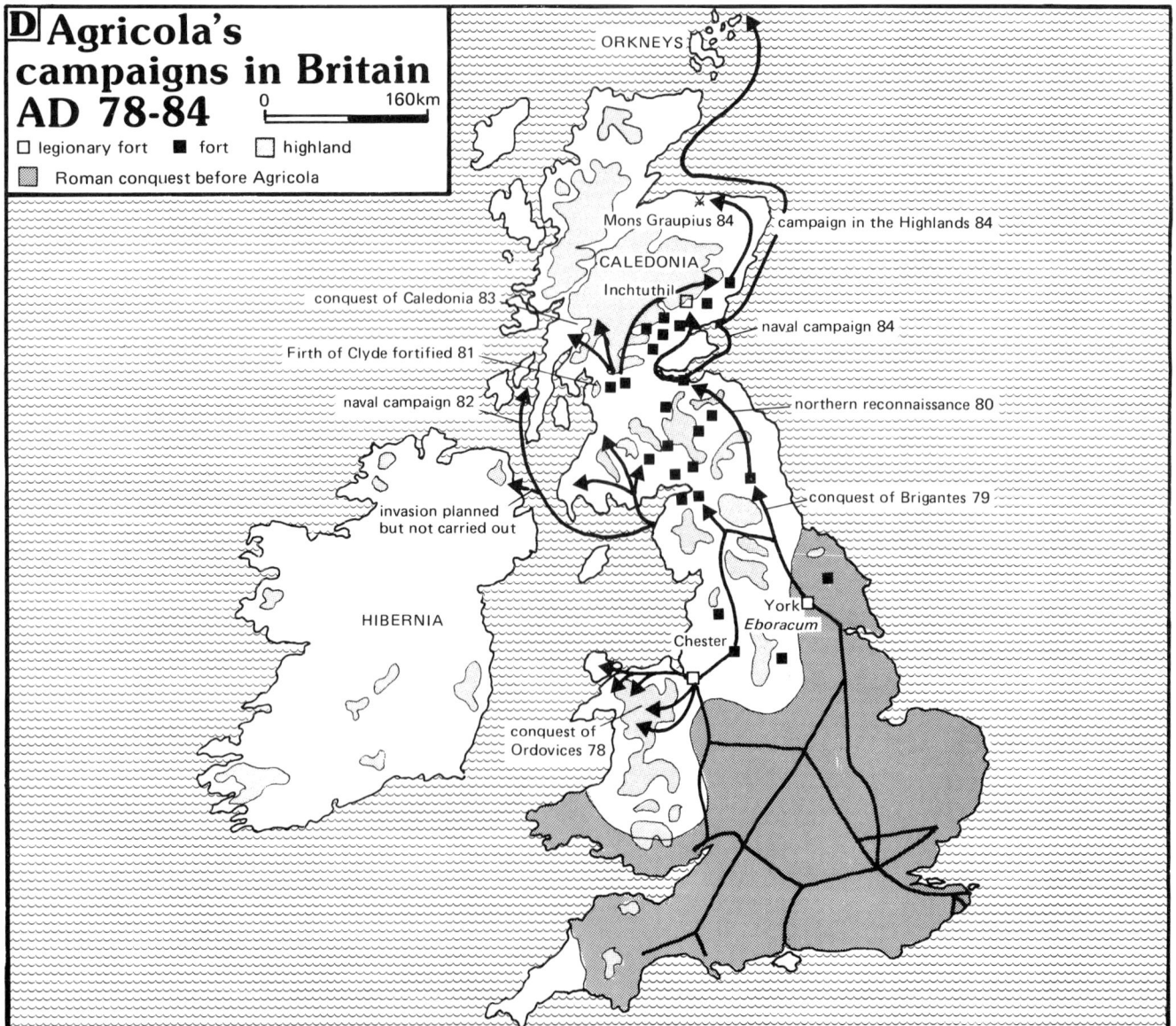

D Agricola's campaigns in Britain AD 78-84

0   160km

□ legionary fort   ■ fort   □ highland

▨ Roman conquest before Agricola

ORKNEYS

Mons Graupius 84 — campaign in the Highlands 84

CALEDONIA

Inchtuthil

conquest of Caledonia 83

naval campaign 84

Firth of Clyde fortified 81

northern reconnaissance 80

naval campaign 82

conquest of Brigantes 79

invasion planned but not carried out

HIBERNIA

York
Eboracum

Chester

conquest of Ordovices 78

From Britain Agricola returned to Rome to do a government job . . . he organized the public games . . . and while not spending too much, he made himself popular. . . Also, he checked gifts to the temples, and ruthlessly tracked down stolen goods. **C**

In AD 77, at the age of thirty-eight, Agricola was made Governor of Britain. **D** shows Agricola's campaigns against the British rebels. Tacitus describes his campaign against a Welsh tribe.

As the Ordovices did not dare come down onto the plain, he led his men up into the hills, himself marching in front so as to spread his courage among the troops by sharing their danger. They cut to pieces almost the whole fighting force of the tribe. . . Agricola also had to deal with new trouble in Anglesey.

He decided to conquer the island. . . As he had thought up the plan quickly, there was no fleet near. Agricola, cunning and determined and knowing the territory, found a way of getting troops across the water. He carefully picked out from his auxiliaries men experienced in wading in shallow waters and trained to swim while carrying their weapons and controlling their horses. He made them throw away all their spare equipment. Then he launched them on a surprise attack. The enemy, who had expected a fleet and a landing, were taken completely by surprise. Who could stop or defeat an enemy who attacked like this? So they asked for peace and surrendered the island. **E**

???????????????????????????????????

1 Write down what thoughts and feelings you might have had as one of Agricola's auxiliaries crossing the Menai Straits. Use these words to help you: chosen, strip off clothes, hold horse, beach, swim, waves, swallow, choke, foothold, dress, enemy, form up, surrender.

2 Use the evidence on these pages to say what qualities Agricola had as a general.

3 To answer this question, you need a map of Wales north of a line from Caernarvon to Shrewsbury. This was the homeland of the Ordovices. Agricola launched his conquest from his base at Chester. How did he make sure that the tribe did not rebel after the conquest? Aerial photographs and archaeologists' excavations of forts, towns and roads give us clues. Agricola did three things: he built

a forts at the mouths of the main rivers on the coast;

b forts near the heads of these main river valleys;

c straight roads, where possible, to link the forts together and to the legionnary fort.

Where do you think Agricola built these? To find out:

i draw your own map of North Wales, showing highlands and rivers;

ii mark where he might have built forts near the river mouths and at their valley heads;

iii draw a network of roads linking the forts together and to Chester (roads will *not* run over highland);

iv write a report on why your forts and roads would have stopped the Ordovices rebelling.

AGRICOLA 2:
the Picts

Over the next six years, Agricola tried to conquer the Pictish tribes. He used ships in his campaigns—a new tactic. They supplied his troops and sometimes landed soldiers behind enemy lines to cut off escape. Finally the Pictish tribes joined together and decided to fight Agricola's army. According to Tacitus, about 30 000 Picts faced Agricola at Mons Graupius. From Tacitus' account of the battle, **A,** we can work out how the two armies were drawn up at its start. See also pages 24-27 for ideas. Agricola held his legions in reserve. The auxiliaries alone fought and won. These tactics had rarely been used before. Photograph **B,** taken from the Pass of Killicrankie, looking down on the battlefield, shows the kind of countryside it was fought in.

The Britons had both guts and skill. With their long swords (C) and small shields, they had the sense to dodge the Roman javelins, and at the same time to hurl a thick volley of their own spears. . . Agricola ordered (five cohorts) to charge the enemy, swords in hand. The Britons were at a disadvantage. Their small shields gave no protection and their long swords with no points were not much use in hand-to-hand fighting. The Batavians (Roman auxiliaries) rushed into the attack with tremendous force. They hacked twice as hard and with their shields pushed back the enemy. They cleared the plain, and began to force their way up the hill in good order. **A**

Meanwhile Pictish chariots pushed back the Roman auxiliary cavalry, and threatened to surround the Roman foot-soldiers. Agricola ordered the four auxiliary cavalry troops that he had kept in reserve to attack the Britons in their rear. The Britons were cut off.

The field was a dreadful sight of blood-shed and destruction. The Britons fled, the Romans chased. They wounded, gashed and mangled the runaways. They grabbed their prisoners and, to be ready for others, butchered them on the spot. . . In one part of the field the Picts, swords in hand, fled in crowds from a handful of Romans; in other parts, without a weapon left, they faced every danger and rushed to certain death. Swords and shields, mangled limbs and dead bodies, covered the plain. The field was red with blood. **D**

Mons Graupius was a final defeat for the Picts. The survivors fled into the Highlands.

When not fighting, Agricola tried to rule Britain fairly—see pages 22-23.

???????????????????????????

1 Imagine that you are high up on the Pass of Killicrankie, watching the battle of Mons Graupius. Write or tape a commentary, using these ideas to help you: the drawing up of the armies; Roman attack; British retreat; cavalry battle; rout of the Britons.

2 Tacitus tells us that Agricola "went in person to mark out the camps, sound the estuaries and explore the woods and forests". His camps had to be near water, on high ground and in the open. Thinking about these points, draw a sketch of **B**, and mark where you would advise Agricola to pitch camp after a day's march?

3 Why do you think Agricola held his legions in reserve? Tacitus says that it was "to save Roman man-power". Is this the whole truth?

4 Tacitus was Agricola's son-in-law. How might this have affected his account?

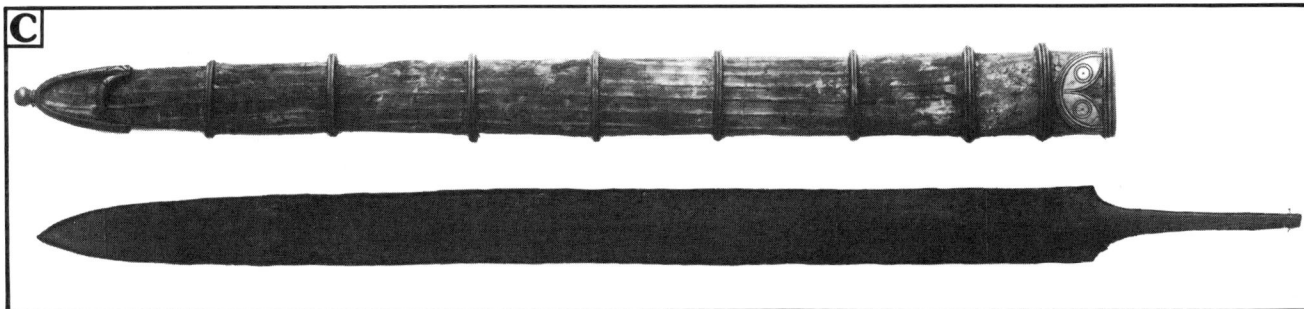

C

BRITISH TRIBES UNDER ROMAN RULE 1

C Roman forts in Trinovantine lands

■ fort

0   30km

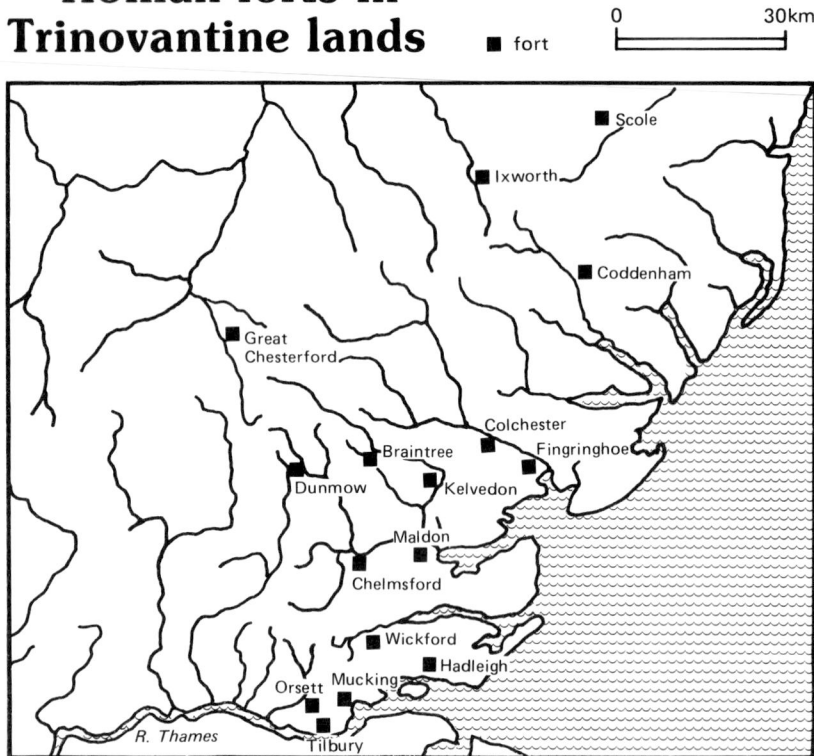

D

What were the Britons like whom the Romans ruled? Remains of British huts and villages that archaeologists have excavated suggest that the Britons were very like those people who lived just across the Channel. This is what Tacitus tells us about them.

When not fighting, the men spend some time hunting, but much more in idleness, doing nothing but eat and sleep. Even the boldest and most warlike have no jobs. Women, old men and weaklings look after the home and fields. . . **A**

It is well known that the people. . . never live in cities. They will not even have their houses close together. They live apart, dotted around, wherever a spring, plain or wood takes their fancy. Their villages are not laid out in the Roman way, with the buildings next to one another. Every man leaves an open space around his house, perhaps because they are such poor builders. They do not even use stones or wall tiles. For everything they use roughly-cut timber, ugly to look at. **B**

Map **C** is based on archaeologists' finds near Colchester—the lands of the Trinovantine tribe. It shows where the Romans might have built forts. **D** is an aerial photograph of one fort.

Map **E** shows where Trinovantine villages and hill forts might have been. Archaeologists have reconstructed tribal homes like the ones they have dug up. **F** is a model of three. It is what Trinovantine huts *might* have looked like.

Tacitus says that a number of villages would join together in a tribe, speaking the same language. The men chose a chief. The tribe met often to discuss problems, judge cases and settle disputes. What did the tribesmen look like?

Everybody in Germany wears a cloak fastened with a brooch or, failing that, a thorn. They pass whole days by their firesides wearing no other clothes. It is a sign of great wealth to wear any garments underneath. . . These garments fit tightly and follow the line of every limb. The people also wear the skins of wild animals. **G**

E **Trinovantine villages and forts**

■ hill fort □ high ground 0   30km
● village T temple

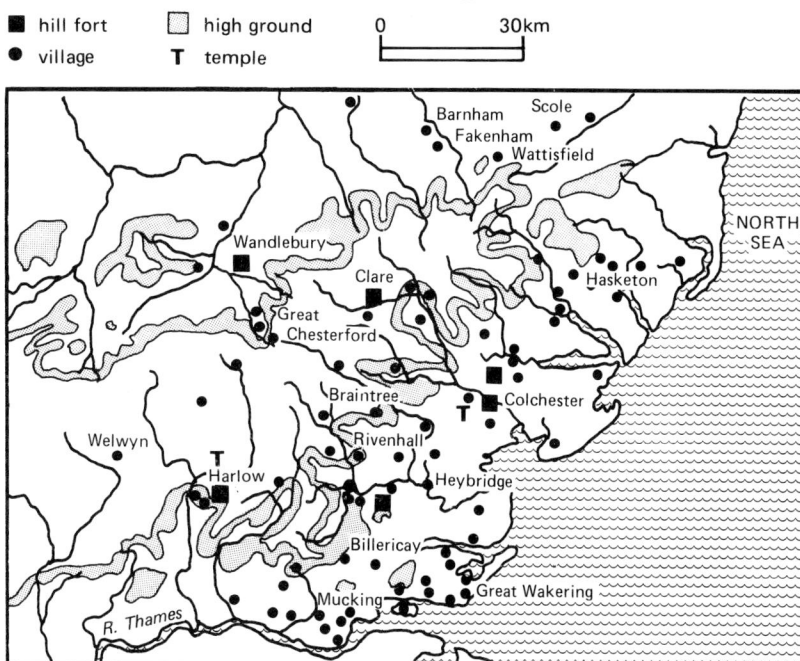

F

???????????????????????????

1 Use the evidence on these pages, and on pages 12-13, to say what the Trinovantine tribe might have been like. Use list **H** to help you.

VILLAGES:
how many there were, why those sites were chosen, what they looked like.
HILL FORTS:
where they were, reason for their sites.

THE TRIBE:
who would have run it, and how.
THE PEOPLE:
what they looked like, how they might have made a living. **H**

2 Look at map **C**. Why do you think the Romans chose these sites for their forts?

3 Look carefully at **D**, and the evidence on pages 28-29. Draw a plan of the fort's walls, gates and buildings.

BRITISH TRIBES UNDER ROMAN RULE 2

C

D

How did the British tribes finally settle down under Roman rule? By the time that the Romans had conquered Britain, they were well practised in ruling defeated people. Tacitus tells us how Agricola dealt with the problem.

He knew how the Britons felt. He had learned from what had happened to others that an army can do little if the government is unfair. He decided to root out the causes of the rebellions. He began with his own men. . . He did not use freedmen or slaves. In choosing centurions and men for his headquarters, he took no notice of his own feelings, nor of recommendations or petitions. Only the best would do—for those he could trust. He knew everything that went on. . . For government jobs he chose men whom he knew would not be greedy—preferring this to punishing greediness. He made the corn tax and money tax less heavy by sharing them out fairly. He put a stop to profiteers' tricks, which were more hated than the taxes themselves. **A**

As well as making sure that the Britons did not hate Roman rule,

Agricola tried to get them to live in peace and quiet instead of fighting. . . He personally backed and gave government help to the building of temples, public squares and good houses. He praised the busy and told off the idle. The Britons' pride in what they were doing was as effective as force.

Further, he gave the sons of chiefs a Roman education, and said that he thought the Britons cleverer than the Gauls. The result was that instead of hating the Roman language (Latin) they were eager to speak it properly. In the same way our national dress became popular. Everywhere you could see togas. So gradually the natives were sucked into the corrupting temptations of shops, baths and rich banquets.

The unsuspecting Britons spoke of such new things as civilization. In fact they were part of their enslavement. **B**

The Romans knew that Britons who learnt Latin also learnt Roman ideas. The Britons' own language was not a written one, so that they could not use it to make records or laws. Roman laws were written down, and had to be obeyed throughout the Empire.

???????????????

1 Use the written EVIDENCE **B**, and map **F**, to make a list of the things that the Romans did to make sure that they ruled peacefully in the lands of, for example, the Durotrigean tribe. Put your list in the order in which you think things happened.

2 Imagine meeting a British chief a hundred years after his great-grandfather surrendered to the Romans. How would he describe points **a-f** in his own lifetime? How would his great-grandfather have described them?

a home;
b clothes;
c language;
d education;
e possessions;
f treatment by Romans.

C is a carving of a British boy and his Roman tutor. **D** shows a diner lying on a couch and being served by a slave, and **E** shows a family. These give us ideas about life under the Romans. Map **F** shows how the Romans settled beside a typical tribe – the Durotriges in southern Britain. The Romans built villas (pages 36-7), towns (pages 38-41) and roads (pages 30-33).

F The pattern of Roman settlement in southern Britain

☐ land over 80 metres ○ town
━ main Roman roads ● farm
▲ pottery kiln △ temple

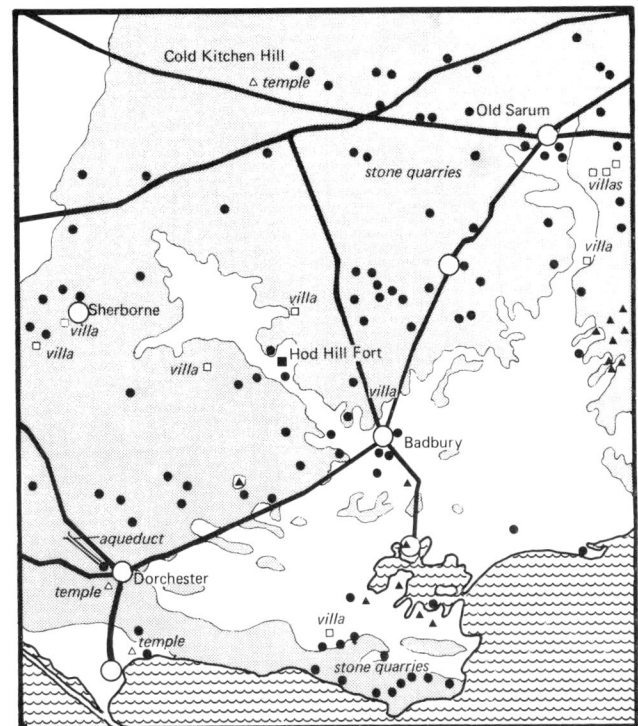

0 5 10 20 km

23

THE ROMAN ARMY 1: Flaminius the legionary

The stone-carver put down his hammer and chisel. On the tombstone he had carved,

Flaminius, son of Titus, of the Pollian tribe from Faventia (Italy), forty-five years old, soldier of the 14th legion called Gemina. I have done my military service and now I am here. **A**

"Here" was the Roman town of Wroxeter, in Shropshire, where Flaminius had lived. We know about him because archaeologists dug up his tombstone, **B**. It is now in the local museum.

Flaminius was a *legionary*—a full-time soldier—in one of more than thirty legions that protected the Roman Empire. His legion invaded Britain in AD 43 and fought with Agricola in Anglesey (see pages 16-17). Each legion had about 5 000 legionaries. Only Roman citizens could become legionaries. Flaminius would have served for twenty-five years. The government paid him a good, regular wage. If his legion won a battle or a campaign, he got a bonus; as he did when a new emperor came to power.

How was Flaminius armed, and how did he fight? Model **C** shows the kind and weight of equipment that a legionary carried. He carried two barbed throwing javelins. He threw the lighter one when the enemy were about fifteen metres away, and the heavier one when they were within ten metres. Even if a javelin missed, its barbs might stick in a Briton's wooden shield, dragging it down. Then the legionary charged. In hand-to-hand fighting Flaminius used a short, stabbing sword, **D**. **E** is a sculptor's idea of legionaries fighting. It is based on drawings, carvings and descriptions of Roman soldiers.

To attack a fort, Flaminius and his comrades would put their shields above their heads. From above they looked like the back of a tortoise. So they called this tactic the tortoise formation (see p. 9).

1 Use the evidence on these pages to make a model, draw, or write about Flaminius. In your work show these things, and say what they were used for.

a Sandals tied with leather straps round his ankles.

b His curved shield with a boss in the middle.

c Short leather trousers, with a wide leather belt.

d Short-sleeved woollen shirt.

e Armour plates worn as a jacket to protect his body.

f Bronze helmet with cheek pieces.

g Short sword carried in its scabbard.

h Javelins.

2 Imagine you were interviewing a soldier in **E**, after the battle. Say what he told you about how the Roman soldiers were equipped and fought, and what had happened in the fight.

C

D

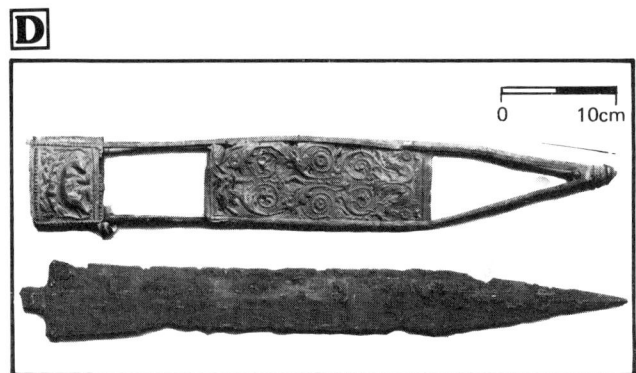

E

THE ROMAN ARMY 2:
a legion's life

How was the army organized, how did it fight and what was life like in it? A *centurion* was in charge of Flaminius. Eighty men made up a *century*. It was split into ten sections. Flaminius and his seven comrades would eat, train and fight together. At night they slept in the same room.

Each legionary belonged to a century; and each century was part of a legion.

This is how the Romans organised a legion for fighting.

2 centuries made up one *maniple*: 160 men.

3 maniples made up one *cohort*: 480 men.

9 cohorts made up one legion (the 1st cohort was twice normal size): 4 800 men.

About 200 cavalry were attached to each legion.

A

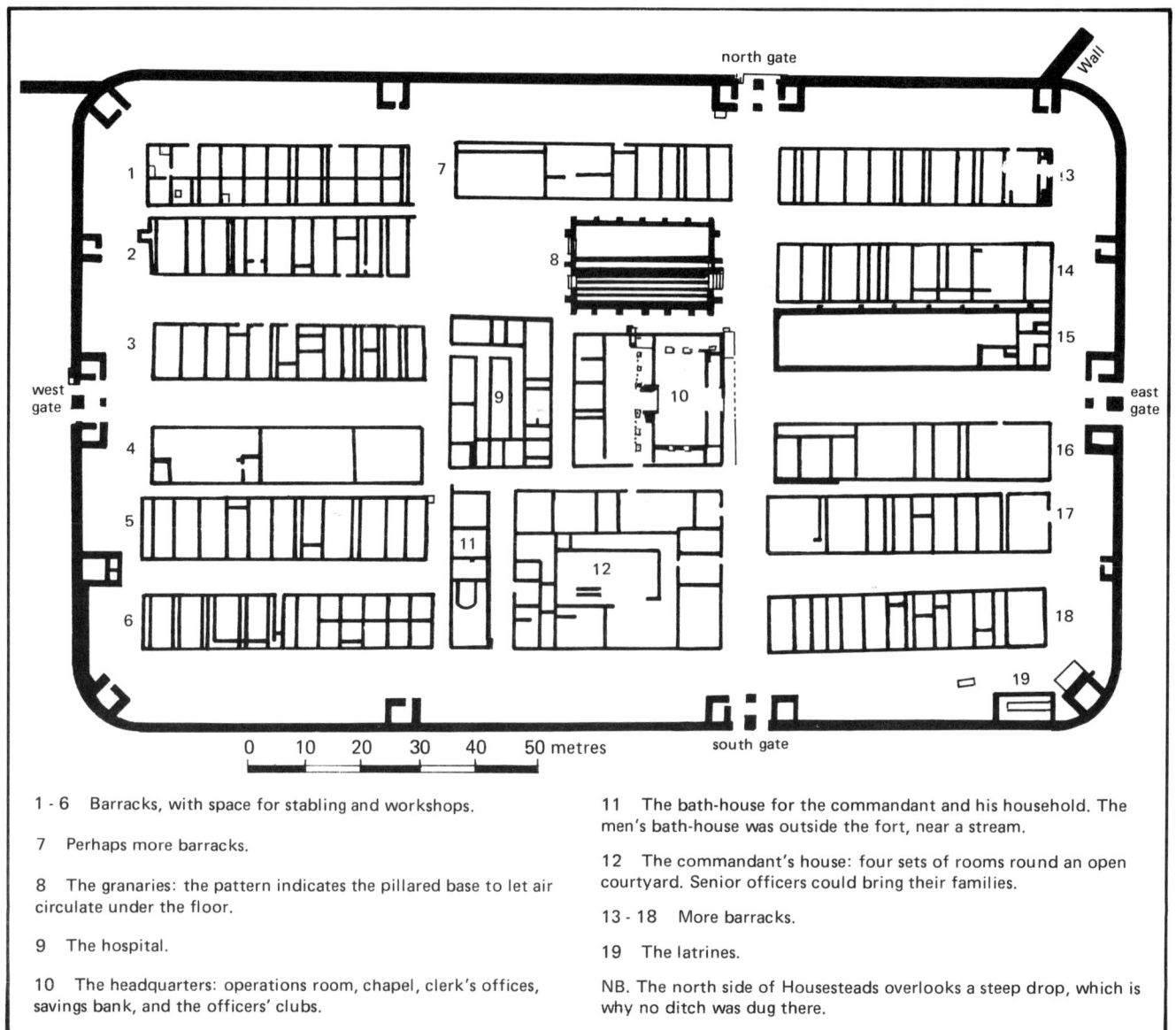

1 - 6   Barracks, with space for stabling and workshops.

7   Perhaps more barracks.

8   The granaries: the pattern indicates the pillared base to let air circulate under the floor.

9   The hospital.

10   The headquarters: operations room, chapel, clerk's offices, savings bank, and the officers' clubs.

11   The bath-house for the commandant and his household. The men's bath-house was outside the fort, near a stream.

12   The commandant's house: four sets of rooms round an open courtyard. Senior officers could bring their families.

13 - 18   More barracks.

19   The latrines.

NB. The north side of Housesteads overlooks a steep drop, which is why no ditch was dug there.

In battle, the legion drew up in two or three lines, with perhaps four cohorts in the front line. The line was between four and eight men deep, a half metre between each man. The gaps between the cohorts in the front line were covered by the second line. This helped the legion to move easily. The cavalry were stationed on the wings.

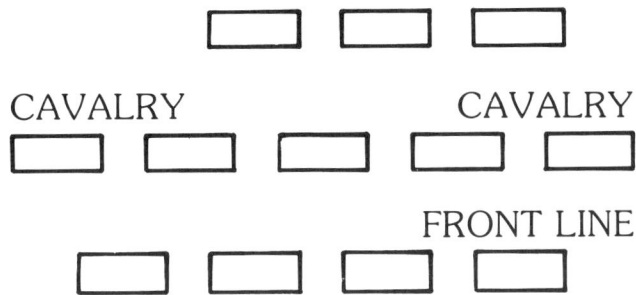

CAVALRY   CAVALRY

FRONT LINE

The training of legionaries was long and expensive. So the Romans were happy to use in their armies warriors from the tribes that they had conquered. These tribesmen – *auxiliaries* – were usually cavalry or archers. The fact that the auxiliaries, although from conquered tribes, fought as free men, often impressed the enemy. Auxiliaries were not allowed to serve in their home area.

On the march, Flaminius would travel up to thirty kilometres a day. Each soldier carried two or three wooden stakes. At night these made a fence round the legion's camp. Much of Flaminius' time was spent in building forts, roads and stone camps. **A** is a plan of a legionary fort on Hadrian's Wall—Housesteads (pages 28-29). He also had to drill each day—to practise marching and obeying battle orders. Mock battles were part of this training. Flaminius used his actual weapons, but covered up the points of his sword and javelins.

After twenty-five years Flaminius retired. Like all soldiers he was given money or a plot of land. His plot was at Wroxeter, and here he died.

1 From the information above, and on pages 24-25, imagine you were interviewing Flaminius after he had retired. Say what he might have told you about his life in the army, and his campaigns.

2 Each legion had an emblem. **B**, a tile from the eaves of a Roman fort, shows one. What is it? Which legion does it belong to? Armies still have emblems, like **C**, from a famous British regiment. Which regiment? What is this emblem used for?

3 Why were auxiliaries not allowed to serve in their home area?

HADRIAN'S WALL

The Roman Emperor, Hadrian, ordered his army in Britain to build a great wall between the Britons in the south and the Picts in the north. The Romans built the wall in AD 120-126 — map **A**.

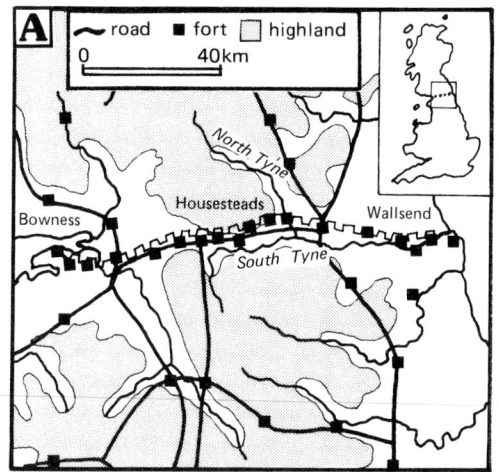

A

B

C

B and **C** are aerial photographs taken on the border. They are some of the evidence that historians use to work out what the defences of Roman Britain were like. On **B**, can you see a ditch about ten metres wide running on the right of the road? Can you also see a ditch immediately to the left of the road?

The excavations of archaeologists are another important sort of evidence. **D-G**, worked out from photographs, excavations and what we know about other Roman walls and forts, give us an idea of how the defences of Hadrian's Wall worked.

The Wall was 117 kilometres long, about 3 metres wide and 6 metres tall. Every 1500 metres there was a small fort for about 30 to 50 soldiers, and a signal tower between each fort. (See **E** and **F**.) The Wall was built of stone, earth and other local materials. Where it ran across low-lying marshy ground, it was made of turf.

G is a model of a small fort. **A**, on pages 26-27, is a plan of a larger fort. Where did the Wall run, as part of the fort?

Every eight kilometres, the Romans built camps for between 500 and 1000 soldiers. Outside the camps native villages grew up, where traders and soldiers' wives lived.

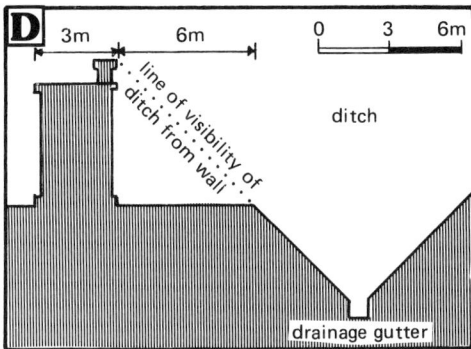

D

3m 6m 0 3 6m

line of visibility of ditch from wall

ditch

drainage gutter

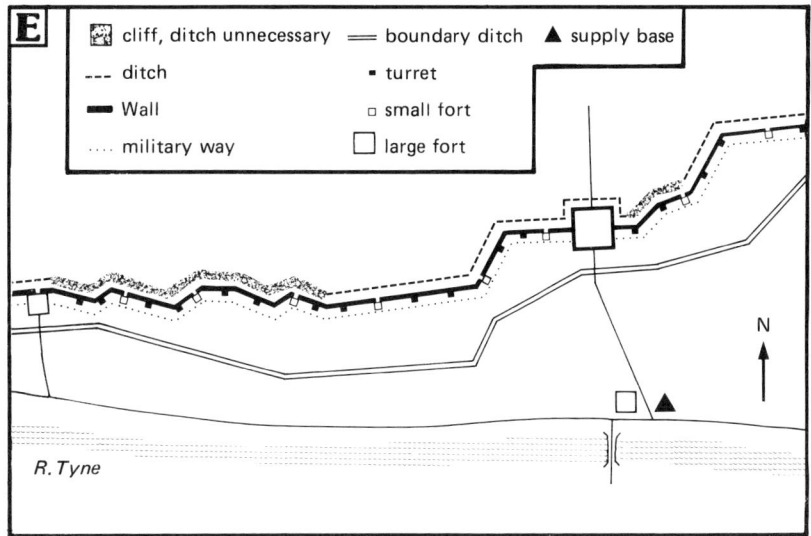

E

cliff, ditch unnecessary	═══ boundary ditch	▲ supply base
--- ditch	▪ turret	
━━ Wall	▫ small fort	
..... military way	☐ large fort	

N

R. Tyne

? ? ? ? ? ? ? ? ?

1 Look at map **A**, and the evidence about Agricola on pages 18-19. Why do you think Hadrian ordered the Wall to be built?

2 What were these features of the Wall used for: ditch in front of wall; forts; signal towers; camps; gates; land cleared behind wall, between it and the rear ditch.

3 Every *metre* of Wall contained *18* cubic metres of stone and earth. Work out the size of the cube which would contain *all* the material used to build the Wall. How long would it take 10 000 men to move this amount of stone and earth?

4 During peacetime, particularly in winter, how did the soldiers in the forts pass their time?

F

G

29

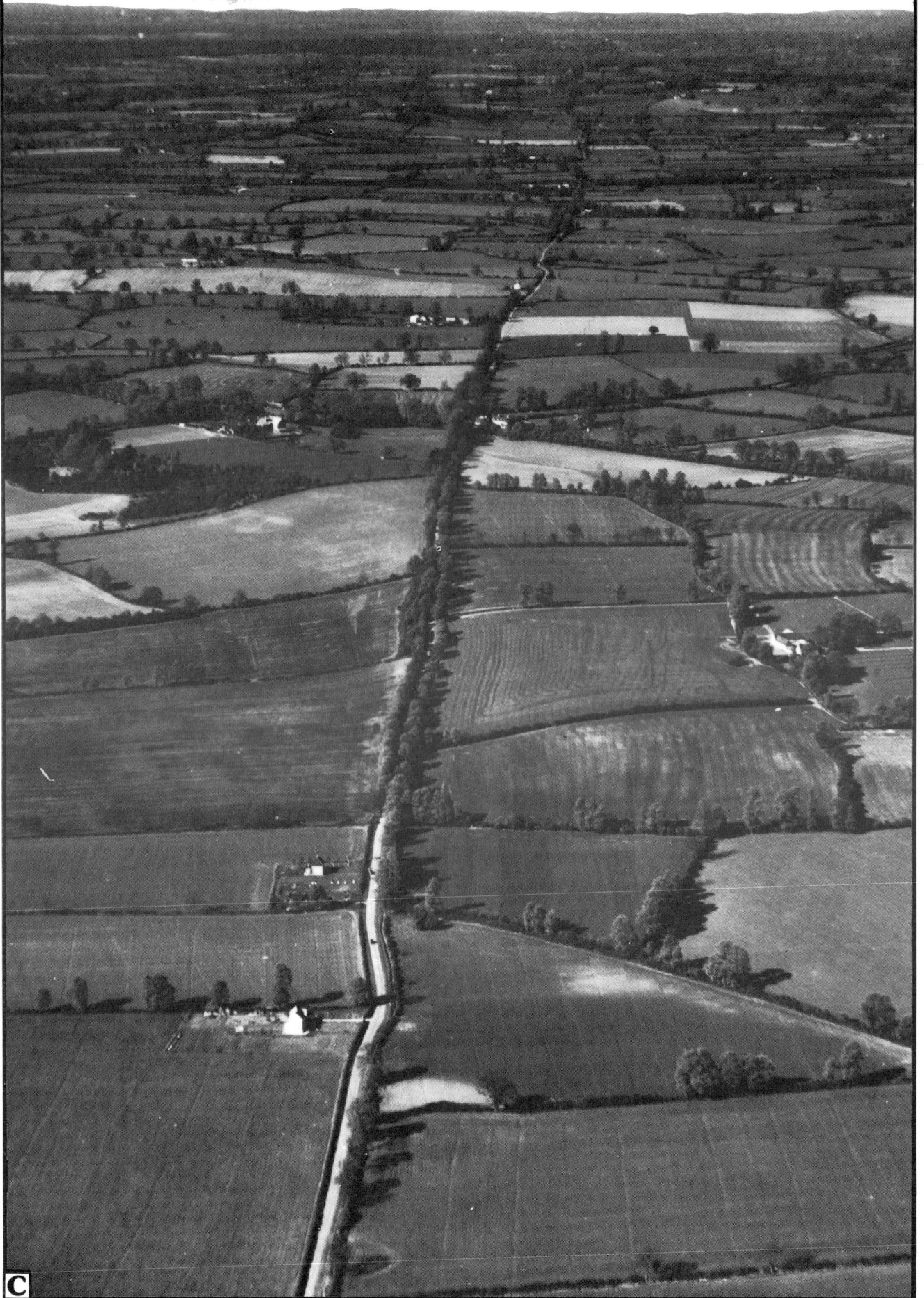

ROMAN ROADS

Roman soldiers were trained engineers. When not fighting, they often had to build roads. A carving on a rock in North Africa tells us that

In the reign of the Emperor Hadrian a battalion from the 6th legion built this road. **A**

Livy, a historian, wrote that

After restoring peace to his province, the Consul Flaminius would not allow soldiers to laze around and made them build a road from Bolgona to Arretium. **B**

Roads linked the Roman Empire together. Most main roads were built—or *fortified*, as the Romans said—so that the army could march quickly to keep the Empire under control **C** is an aerial photograph of a Roman road. Roads also increased trade. This meant more taxes for the Roman Emperor. In Britain, important industrial areas, like the lead- and silver-mining districts of Somerset and Derbyshire, had good roads.

Roads helped ideas to spread across the Empire: for example, the spread of Christianity across Britain in the 7th century. They saved travellers much time. Travellers had to pay tolls for using the roads. Traders had to pay different sums for different goods: for example, much more for a slave than a goat. Roman officials paid nothing, and got free lodgings and fresh horses at government hostels along main roads. They used the hostels as government "post offices".

Travellers on the roads spread disease through the Empire. But plants and flowers which grew by the roadside were used in medicine.

Could there be a Roman road near where you live? Place-names can give us evidence about these roads: for example *strat*, as in Stratford, meaning stony, was the name later given to Roman roads by the Saxons.

???????????

1 Use an atlas to find other examples of place-names that suggest the presence of Roman roads.

2 Do you know of any roads and bridges where tolls are still charged?

3 Look carefully at **C**, and work out the route of the straight Roman road? List the reasons why the Romans chose that route.

4 When roads needed repairing, the local tribes had to find the money. Why did the Romans think this a good idea?

5 You can use Map **B**, pages 44-45, to find out which towns were the most important to the Romans. Count the roads that each town has running to it. Then list the towns in order of those with most roads, the second most and so on. The town with the most roads will be of the *first* rank, the one or ones with the second most of the *second* rank, and so on.

TOWN	NO OF ROADS	RANK

31

BUILDING A ROMAN ROAD

How did the Romans go about building their roads?

First, surveyors planned the route. Usually they chose *a straight line*—the shortest distance—but not always. They would aim at high points in the landscape, for from one high point to the next they could check whether the road was going straight in the right direction. The surveyors preferred dry, level ground, or ground called *the military crest*, just below the top of a slope, where soldiers could see without being seen. The engineers often cleared trees from the roadside to give better warning of attack. These things helped to avoid ambush.

The engineers used local materials, so that not all roads were alike. Most main roads had a curved surface and side ditches for drainage. They had a solid base made of stones, and the top was finished with gravel or similar material. **A** shows part of a road across the Pennines. **B** is an artist's idea of how it was probably built.

Soldiers, slaves and local tribesmen carried out the work. Tacitus wrote that the Pictish chieftain Calgacus complained that

Our money is carried into their treasury and our corn into their granaries. Our limbs and bodies build roads through swamps and woods. And what do we get—blows and insults. **C**

Often the builders needed guards.

A

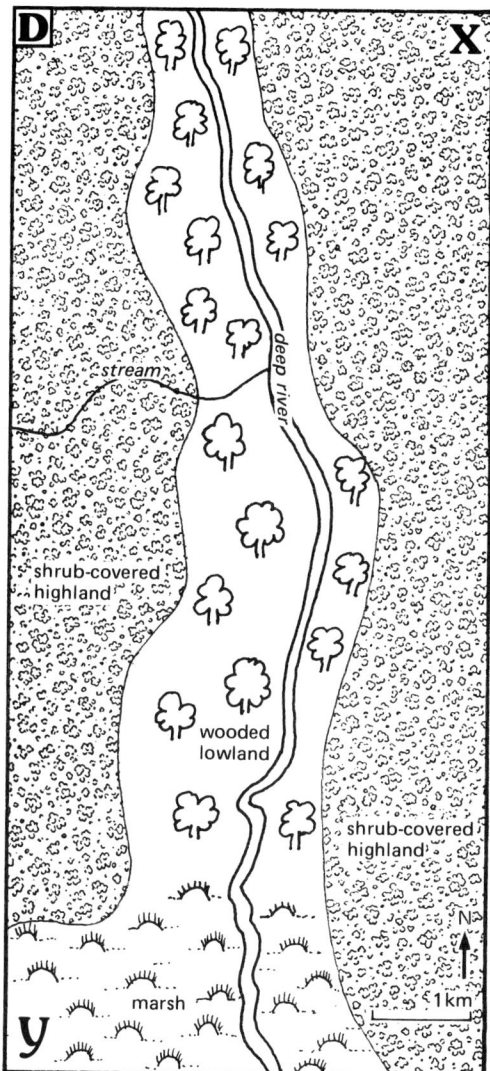

Map D

- X
- deep river
- stream
- shrub-covered highland
- wooded lowland
- shrub-covered highland
- N
- 1km
- marsh
- y

B

???????????????????????????

1 Why was there a deep groove in the centre of the road **A**?

2 Why did the builders need guards?

3 What road-building material would the Romans have used in your area?

4 Map **D**, shows an area just conquered by a Roman army. Imagine you are a Roman engineer who has to build a road from x to y across the map. You have to plan a route. Take into account points **a-f**.

a It should be as straight as possible.

b It should be on dry, *level* ground, *or* the military crest.

c It should aim at high points, to give a good view.

d You must clear trees 100 metres on each side.

e You will need a bridge across the river.

f You must build a hostel for government messengers and horses halfway along the road.

Make a copy of the map, and mark in the route of your road. Then, draw a cross-section of your road, and label it to show the way you have designed it.

THE COUNTRYSIDE 1:
plants
and animals

The Romans brought many plants to Britain. They introduced new crops, such as rye, oats and flax; and some new vegetables such as cabbage, carrots, celery and turnips. They also brought parsnips, which helped to feed farm animals in winter and saved them from having to be killed. The Romans planted stinging nettles. They introduced plum, apple, walnut and cherry trees. We know this because archaeologists found no trace of these trees before the Romans came. Four of the flowers that they planted in their gardens were the rose, pansy, lily and poppy.

The Romans also brought with them different kinds of animal. Oxen pulled their wagons, because only they had necks strong enough to take the strain, by heavy wooden yokes. It takes a long time to train oxen. If you give them too heavy a load to start with, they sit down and stay there. You must start with a small load, and gradually increase the weight. **A** shows the training of a team of oxen today.

Roman horses and cattle were bigger than those of the Britons. After the Romans left Britain, the cattle roamed wild through the English forests. The bulls were hunted for sport until three hundred years ago. Now they are rare. You can see a herd of white cattle like those of the Romans at the Cotswold Farm Park.

The Romans improved the quality of sheep in Britian. British woollen goods became famous throughout the Empire. Tunics made from sheep's wool were very popular. Also, Tacitus wrote that

The Britons were famous for a cloak called birrus Britannicus. *It was woollen and kept off rain very well.*   **B**

Romans also introduced the edible dormouse. They kept them in special cages, and fattened them on chestnuts and poppy seeds. Petronius, a Roman writer, described a feast in **C**. **D** is from a cookbook by Apicius.

There were small iron frames shaped like bridges, on which lay dormice sprinkled with honey and poppy seed.   **C**

Stuff the dormice with minced pork pounded with pepper, pine kernels and sauce. Sew up, place on a tile and put in the oven to cook.   **D**

34

1 Why did the Romans plant stinging nettles?

2 The Romans did not use their cattle for food, but for another purpose. What do you think it was?

3 How do we know that Roman horses and cattle were larger than those of the Britons? How might their size have helped the Romans?

4 What is your favourite meal? Compare the way it is cooked with the preparation of the edible dormouse.

5 Look at the plants and trees that the Romans introduced, **E**. How many can you recognize near your school or home? If the Romans had not introduced them, how different would your environment be?

E

Rose

Lily

Poppy

Pansy

Walnut

Plum

Cherry

Apple

THE COUNTRYSIDE 2: farming

A

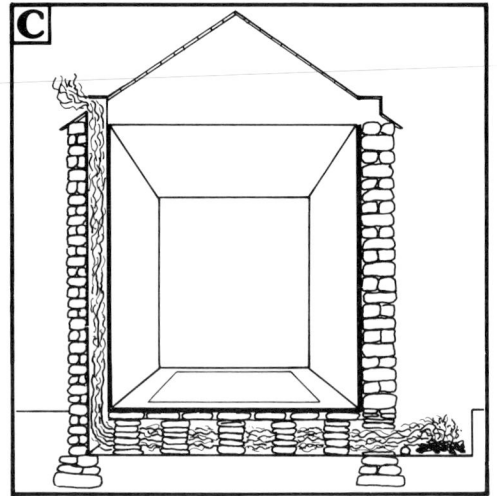

C

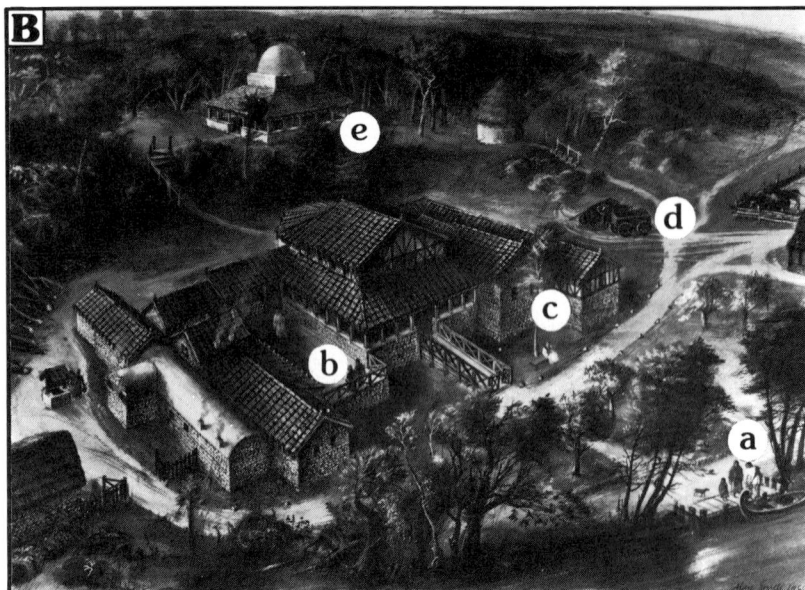

B

D

If Flaminius had gone from Wroxeter to visit a friend in Silchester, he would have come across land cleared for growing crops. Farmers had to give about a twelfth of their harvest to the Emperor. The richer Roman settlers built large farmhouses—villas—in the middle of their farms. Archaeologists have found over a hundred villas in Britain. **A** shows their excavations at one. **B** is an artist's reconstruction of the villa at Lullingstone, Kent.

What was life like in a villa? A major problem was to keep warm in cold weather. **C** shows how the Romans heated their homes. *Hypocausts* sometimes made the floors so hot that people had to wear thick-soled shoes. **D** shows the mosaic floor of a hypocaust. It is made of small coloured tiles set in concrete in a pattern. In the villa-owners's living-room, artists painted pictures on the plastered walls. Most Britons could not afford villas. They either still lived in round huts, or built rectangular ones.

E, F, G and **H** give an idea of some of the jobs done on the farm at different seasons. The owner of Lullingstone used slaves to do the hard work. Throughout the Empire, slaves were vital in running farms and industries. Some loyal and hard-working slaves were given their freedom. Most were treated as we treat horses today. Archaeologists discovered evidence in a Buckinghamshire villa, about how the Romans treated unwanted slaves. Altogether they found the skeletons of ninety-seven new-born baby girls.

E

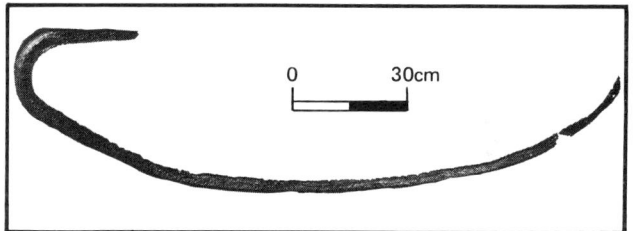
F

G

H

??????????????

1 Make a list of what the slaves are doing in pictures **E, G** and **H**. What does **F** show?

2 Imagine that you had walked with Flaminius down a minor road to Lullingstone villa. The owner showed you around his farmhouse. Say what he might have pointed out at points **a, b, c, d** and **e** of picture **B**.

3 Use the information above, and on pages 34-35, to make out a table of the kind of crops in the Lullingstone fields in July, the trees in the orchards, the animals on the farm and the herbs in the garden.

4 What do you think happened to the ninety-seven girl babies and why?

5 Using this book, say from what kinds of evidence the artist of **B** might have worked out what Lullingstone looked like.

THE TOWN

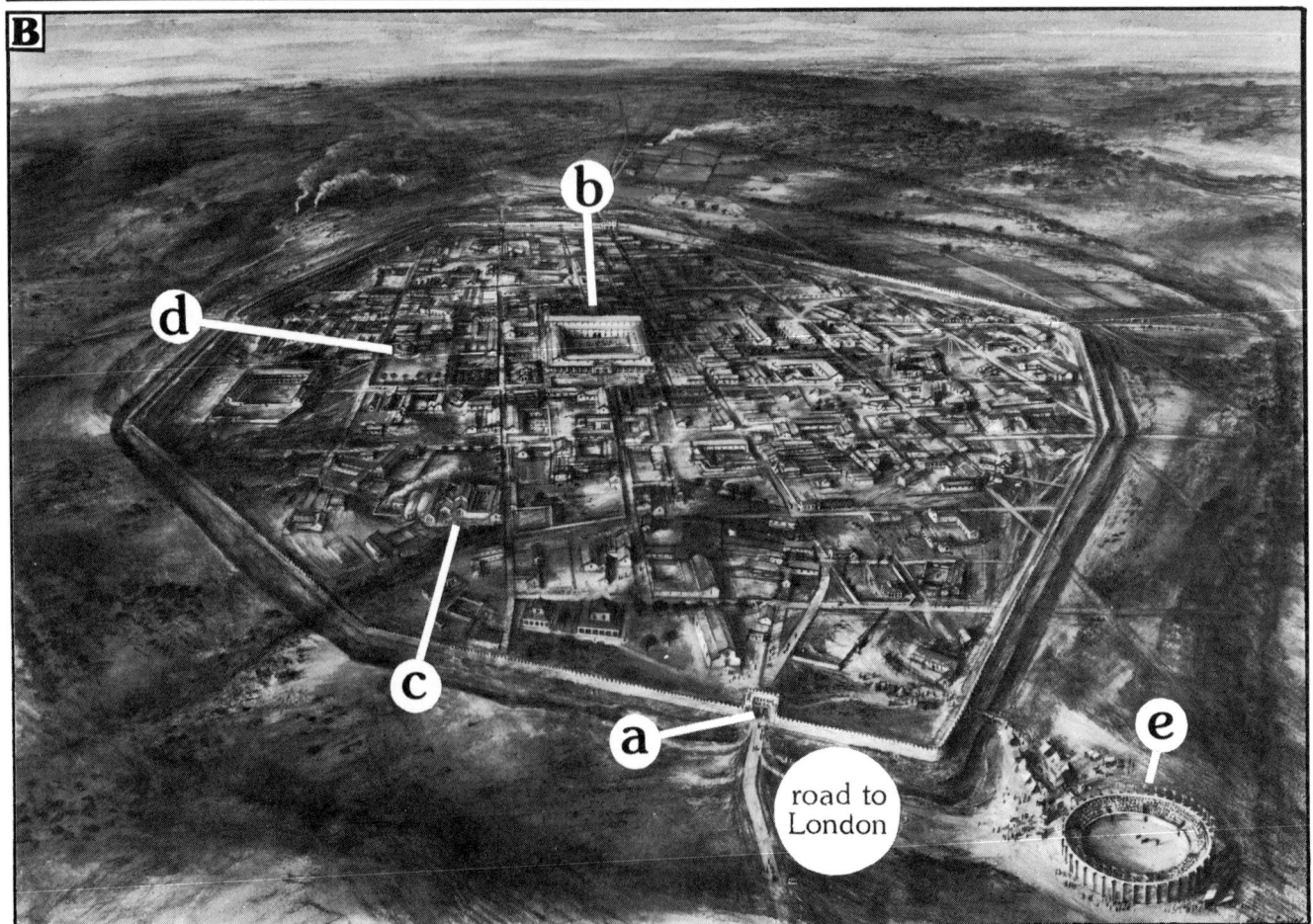

road to
London

At the end of the Roman road from Wroxeter, Flaminius reached the Roman town of Silchester. The Romans built their towns either as army bases, or in the middle of the lands of a conquered tribe, or as a settlement—colony—for retired soldiers—veterans.

Archaeologists have excavated Roman towns in Britain, such as Wroxeter and Silchester. **A** is an aerial photograph of Silchester today. **B** is an artist's reconstruction of what Silchester might have looked like. Towns like Silchester provided services for the townspeople and the surrounding tribesmen. **C, D, E** and **F** show some of the shops in a country town. The Romans built roads into the countryside, to serve their villas and farms. The farmers took their produce by road to the town, where they bought the goods they needed for life on the farm.

Roman towns were planned on a grid of roads, looking like a chessboard from above. In the central squares were the most important buildings—the baths, the temple and the *basilica* or headquarters of local government. In the outer

1 Make out a shopping list of the things that you could buy in **C, D, E** and **F**. Say what the shops were like, and where they might have got their goods from.

2 Why did the Romans let the tribes elect their own councils? Who would the tribes pick?

3 Use **B** to draw a plan of the shape of Silchester. Use **A** to mark where the streets were. Why do you think they show up on the aerial photograph? Also mark on your plan the buildings shown on **B**, points **a-e**.

squares the Romans built shops and houses like **G**.

The basilica was on one side of the main square—*forum*. Here met the council which ran the affairs of the town and the local tribe. The Romans let the Britons choose their own councils. In the courts of the basilica, *magistrates* tried cases and settled disputes. Magistrates were usually Roman citizens.

TOWN LIFE

D

How would Flaminius have passed his spare time in Silchester? Outside many towns was an arena, often built around a hollow in the ground. There the Romans held plays or fights between gladiators—slaves who fought one another to entertain the public. **A** is the site of the Dorchester arena. **B** is a mosaic of fighting gladiators.

Flaminius would have visited the baths to meet friends and relax and to talk business. When he had undressed, he would rub oil into his skin. Then a slave would use a *strigil* to scrape off the dirt in a very hot sweat room. The Romans had no soap. Then Flaminius would jump into the cold, plunge bath. A Roman writer, Seneca tells us that

. . . people jump into the bath with a mighty splash. . . along comes the drink-seller with his whole range of cries, the sausage-seller and the pastry-man. . . **C**

D shows the reconstructed remains of a plunge bath, in the town of Bath, which people used until very recently.

???????????????

1 Imagine that you walked with Flaminius around Silchester. Describe what you saw, heard, smelled and did at these places: gate, basilica, baths, shops, house of Flaminius' friend, gladiators' fight in the arena, temple.

2 Using the evidence on pages 38-39, say what different services towns like Silchester provided for both Romans and Britons in the town and surrounding tribal area. How far do you think the town's influence spread?

41

INDUSTRY AND TRADE

What were the tiles on the roofs of Lullingstone villa and the houses in Silchester made of? Where did the lead for water pipes come from, and the iron for Flaminius' armour and weapons? Who made the pottery used in every Roman house?

Map **A** shows the sites of Roman mines and works so far discovered. All minerals belonged to the Emperor. So at first the army ran the mines and quarries, and worked them by forced labour. In the Mendip mines, slaves and convicts lived and died in underground chambers. Later, private businessmen were allowed to run mines, provided they gave half the produce to the Emperor.

Lead was the most important mining industry. Refined lumps of lead—pigs—are still dug up near the Snailbeach mines, in Shropshire. Pliny, a Roman writer, said:

Lead is made into pipes and thin sheets. It is mined with some difficulty in Spain and Gaul, but in Britain it is present in such quantity near the surface that there is a law to limit the amount mined. **B**

The Romans also mined copper and tin, and mixed and smelted them to make bronze jewellery and tools. They mixed tin with lead to make pewter dishes and cups. Iron tools became more common.

They made pottery wherever they found suitable clay.

The slave trade itself was big business, and many British slaves were sold abroad. Slaves were a good cargo—they moved themselves about.

???????????????????

1 Where would a Roman trader have got these things from: tin, copper, lead, silver, iron, pottery? What would he have used them for?

2 Why was the slave trade important to the Romans?

3 How did the Romans refine the salt from their salt-works on the coast?

4 At first, the Romans only conquered lowland Britain. Why did they soon want the highlands as well?

A Roman mines and works

☐ highland   ● town   ■ legionary fort   0   160km

Hadrian's Wall
Lead Coal
Lead Pottery
■ YORK
Iron
Coal LINCOLN
Copper Lead Lead Salt
■ CHESTER Pottery
Coal Stone Salt
Copper ○ LEICESTER Salt
Pottery Pottery
Pottery ● CAISTOR
Gold
Iron ST ALBANS
CAERLEON ■ ● GLOUCESTER LONDON Salt
Coal SILCHESTER
Lead Stone Iron
Coal ● BATH
Lead Mendip Hills
Pottery
EXETER PURBECK
Marble
DORCHESTER Shale
Tin

42

THE GODS

The Romans worshipped many different gods. **A** and **B** show the stone heads of two of them: Minerva, the goddess of wisdom, and Mithras, the god of the sun.

Romans worshipped in temples. The head of Minerva was discovered at Bath in the temple named after Sulius Minerva. We think that Sulius was a British goddess—whom the Romans said was the same person as Minerva.

Archaeologists found the head of Mithras in the ruins of a Roman temple in London. The head was *hidden* in the ruins.

C shows the remains of a Roman temple on Hadrian's Wall. Here Roman soldiers worshipped a *British* god, Antenociticus.

In their temples the Romans sacrificed animals to the gods. They hoped that in return the gods would help them in their lives.

By AD 400, the Romans had given up their old gods. The worship of Jesus Christ spread from the Middle East. At first the Roman emperors had tried to stamp out the worship of Christ, but later they became Christians as well.

In about AD 730, a British monk wrote about the struggles of the British Christians against their Roman rulers in about AD 300.

In the same attacks (on Christians) suffered Aaron and Julius . . . and many others of both sexes. After they had endured many horrible tortures, death ended the struggle. Their souls then entered the joys of the heavenly city. When this storm of attacks ended, faithful Christians came out into the open and rebuilt the ruined churches. They had hidden in woods, lonely places and secret caves during the troubles. **D**

???????????

1 Why did the Romans worship Minerva and Mithras?

2 Can you think why the head of Mithras was hidden?

3 Why did Roman soldiers on Hadrian's Wall worship a native god? Did they worship this god privately or in groups?

4 Does the evidence about Sulius Minerva and Antenociticus suggest anything to you about how and why the Britons were happy to accept Roman rule?

5 Look at page 37, **D**. The symbol behind the head stands for the first letters of the Greek world Christos. What does the mosaic show? Why did Christians use secret symbols?

THE END OF ROMAN BRITAIN

In AD 367, the Roman Emperor Valentian, in Germany, read his letters from Britain. The news was very bad indeed.

Barbarians were plundering Britain. They had killed General Nectardius, in charge of the coast. They had ambushed and taken prisoner another General, Fullofaudes. **A**

B Roman forts, towns and roads

☐ highland   ■ legionary fort   ● town   — road

0   150km

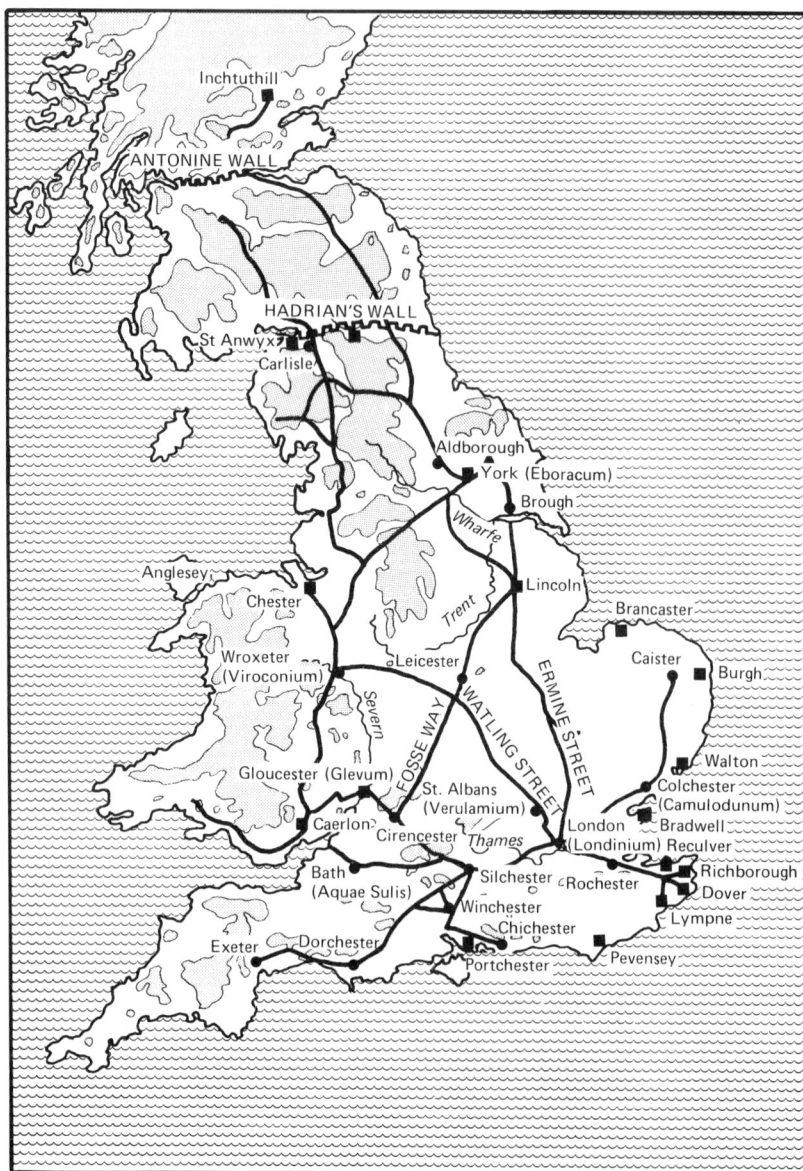

Inchtuthill
ANTONINE WALL
HADRIAN'S WALL
St Anwy x?
Carlisle
Aldborough
York (Eboracum)
Brough
Wharfe
Anglesey
Chester
Trent
Lincoln
Brancaster
Wroxeter (Viroconium)
Leicester
Caister
Burgh
Severn
FOSSE WAY
WATLING STREET
ERMINE STREET
Walton
Gloucester (Glevum)
St. Albans (Verulamium)
Colchester (Camulodunum)
Caerleon
Cirencester
Thames
London (Londinium)
Bradwell
Reculver
Bath (Aquae Sulis)
Silchester
Rochester
Richborough
Dover
Winchester
Lympne
Chichester
Pevensey
Exeter
Dorchester
Portchester

Who were these invaders? In the north of England, Pictish warriors broke through the defences of Hadrian's Wall. In the west, Irish raiders landed. The south-east was attacked by raiders who sailed across from the Rhine Delta. All of them came to steal and destroy. Soon they penetrated the centre of Roman Britain.

How were the Romans to stop the raiders? Valentian decided to build large forts and towers—map **B**. Look particularly at those along the coast from Norfolk to Hampshire. They were bases for both ships and soldiers. The Romans called them the forts of the Saxon shore. **C** is an aerial photograph of Portchester Castle, a Saxon shore fort. The Normans built a castle in one corner, an abbey in the other.

The Roman military engineer would have had in mind points **a-d** when he advised the local commander where to build these forts.

a The forts must be on the coast, so that the Roman fleet could cut off invaders when they landed.
b They must be at the mouth of a river, up which raiders might sail in their small, flat-bottomed boats.
c They must be from fifteen to twenty kilometres apart.
d They must be within ten kilometres of any one of the towns shown.

C

How did the Britons feel about these attacks? In about AD 550, one of them wrote:

. . . all the columns (of the town) were knocked to the ground by many strokes of the battering ram, all the farmers were driven away, together with the bishops, priests and people. Meanwhile the sword shone and the flames crackled on every side . . . **D**

E shows the remains of a Roman tower at Dover. An artist has based drawing **F** on the remains of towers like this, and on similar buildings that have survived from Roman times.

For the next hundred years, raiders continued to land on Britain's coast. The barbarian attacks on Britain were only part of many attacks on the Roman Empire in the Western Europe. In AD 401, the Emperor took many of the troops from Britain to defend Rome. By 410 nearly all the soldiers had left. The Emperor told the Romans in Britain that they would have to look after themselves.

Maps **C** and **E** on pages 20-21 show Trinovantine tribe's lands in AD 400. If you had been born in Colchester in that year, what might you have seen in the next fifty years as Roman rule collapsed in Britain? List **G** gives an idea of what went on as Roman troops left Britain to defend Italy.

a Some soldiers leave.

b News is heard of barbarian raids on villas.

c Roman farmers and their families leave villas more than ten kilometres from the towns.

45

E

F

d Less food is grown. Fewer goods are sold in the town to people who live in the surrounding villas and villages.

e Shops and workshops in the town begin to close.

f The rest of the soldiers leave. The forts are empty. The Britons try to train soldiers to fight the invaders.

g Raiders move closer to the town. Most villas are deserted.

h Little food is grown. Very few goods are made and sold in the town's shops.

i Disease breaks out in the town. Most people die.

j The town is almost empty. Nearly all the villas are in ruins. **G**

??????????????

1 Look carefully at **E** and **F**. We know that these towers were not forts and that a Roman fleet had its base twenty kilometres away across the Channel, at Boulogne. What do you think the towers were for?

2 Look at pages 36-37. Say what you might have seen on a trip around the villa, its buildings and fields ten years after the last Roman and his native workers had fled. Visit points **a-e**, in **B**, page 36.

3 How did Roman rule over Britain end? Why do you think it did?